From the Natural Man to the Political Machine

Gabriela Ratulea

From the Natural Man to the Political Machine

Sovereignty and Power in the Works of Thomas Hobbes

PETER LANG
EDITION

Bibliographic Information published by the Deutsche Nationalbibliothek
The Deutsche Nationalbibliothek lists this publication in the Deutsche Nationalbibliografie; detailed bibliographic data is available in the internet at http://dnb.d-nb.de.

Library of Congress Cataloging-in-Publication Data
Ratulea, Gabriela, 1969-
From the natural man to the political machine : sovereignty and power in the works of Thomas Hobbes / Gabriela Ratulea. – Peter Lang edition.
pages cm
Includes bibliographical references.
ISBN 978-3-631-66550-3 – ISBN 978-3-653-05889-5 (E-Book)
1. Hobbes, Thomas, 1588-1679–Political and social views. 2. Political science–Philosophy. 3. Power (Social sciences)–Philosophy. 4. Sovereignty. 5. Natural law. I. Title.
JC153.H52R37 2015
320.01–dc23
2015018535

ISBN 978-3-631-66550-3 (Print)
E-ISBN 978-3-653-05889-5 (E-Book)
DOI 10.3726/978-3-653-05889-5

Peter Lang – Frankfurt am Main · Bern · Bruxelles · New York · Oxford · Warszawa · Wien

This publication has been peer reviewed.

www.peterlang.com

Table of contents

Introduction

As John Rawls has pointed out, the modern moral and political philosophy begins with Hobbes, and with the reaction to Hobbes. Usually there is a tendency to oppose Thomas Hobbes to the liberal thinkers and to consider him as the theoretician of the unlimited political power. Nevertheless the main problem is similar in Hobbes's theory as well as in liberal theory, their common question being: how is the rational freedom possible and how to guarantee the exercise of civic duties of citizens? This is the reason why we should consider the opposition between Hobbes and liberals as not to being found in their aspirations, since both theories aim for a society in which individuals enjoy their freedom without expose to danger the safety of their fellows. The opposition is merely to be found at the level of means of action which are considered for attaining this objective: unlimited political power *versus* limited political power. Hobbes and the entire liberal view consider that a liberal political society must be founded on moral facts and properties. These moral resources, which are not necessarily of religious inspiration, are coming from the *foro interno* of individuals and prevent them from doing certain actions. But the individual moral sense is not efficient and sufficient in all the circumstances to insure the stability of any given society. For this reason, it is necessary to impose some external limits which are able to compel the individuals to respect some moral rules, and this action is to be done by political power.

Approaching the *Leviathan* to the liberal ideology (whose founder is considered to be John Locke) we may say, as some interpreters did (like Leo Strauss or C. A. Macpherson), that modern individualism begins, in theory, with the intellectual work of Hobbes. "Although his conclusions barely can be considered as liberals, its postulates are deeply individualistic,"[1] since he deduces political rights and obligations from the interests and the will of separate individuals. His conceptions of society, justice and natural law would be traditional, but the foundation of political rights and obligations is to be understood in connection with two major suppositions: the equality of needs and the equal insecurity. Also, for him, the moral rely on politics and has its origins in the social contract and the birth of civil society.

During the civil war (1640–1649) it appeared to Hobbes that people's security and well-being cannot be guaranteed in the state of anarchy or in the absence of

1 C. B. Macpherson, *The political Theory of Possessive Individualism Hobbes to Locke* (London: Oxford University Press, 1964), p. 1.

a *real* political power capable to solve the conflicts that inevitably rise in a given human society. In this respect the *Leviathan* is not only a philosophical, but also a juridical and moral answer to the political crisis generated by the civil war. The English philosopher develops in his political theory the only efficient solution to the problem of violence and war: the institution of an absolute and powerful political government. Only such a power can restore the order there where violence dominates and can prevent the violence there where order still reigns. We may say today that Hobbes sustains the capacity of government at the expense of democratic institutions, but we could not blame him since he invented the idea of legitimacy of politics in the modern sense, when he stated that even the sovereignty by acquisition is founded "not by the victory, but by the consent of the vanquished."

In Hobbes's view, the role of the state it is not to create or promote a virtuous life for people, but to defend every one's natural right. In this respect, natural and civil law are closely related to each other. The main function of positive law is therefore to apply natural law, not to declare it void. Natural laws such as equity, justice and gratitude pertain to those moral features which determine people to search for peace; they become effective laws only within the state. If natural law is part of civil law in every civil state, civil law is, in its turn, part of natural law as long as the observance of the conventions and the commandment to give to every man his own are precepts of natural law. Therefore, there are no fundamental differences between natural and civil laws, since they are just different aspects of the only general law, one being unwritten, the other written. Despite these remarks, the right to natural liberty may be restraint by civil laws, as long as these laws are made to provide peace and security, so that people do not harm each other, but help each other and be united against a common enemy. The possibility for a rational and consequently a peaceful order to prevail is given by the sovereign's absolute power, and this is because he is the only person who keeps integrally the natural precepts.

In Hobbes's theory, the laws that lead to the institution of the civil society are all deduced from the concept of human nature. Thus, the concept of *human nature* is not only a descriptive or an explaining concept, but it is outstandingly a boundary-concept.[2] The state of nature, it is not the state of the beginning, it is deeply embedded in the psychological characteristics of the mankind, being on the one hand synonym of danger that threats continually the humanity and pursue it from the shadow, and on the other hand the principle of virtue and the condition of possibility of common good.

---

2 Or, more accurately, a limiting concept, the *Grenzbegriff* of which Kant speaks.

If we consider the international political situation of this early 21st century, we are entitled to assert that the technological transformations of the art of war created a new equality in insecurity among people. The crisis of sovereignty in some societies produces new dangers for the global security. This is the reason why, through the realist school of thought in International Relations, Hobbes's political theory could indicate some principle of action, in connection with the liberal theory. Hobbes was that thinker of the 17th century who founded the rational political obligation on the human nature itself. His realistic assumptions could help the contemporary people to understand that there is no liberty where there is no political authority.

Chapter 1: Hobbes in Context

In order to understand Hobbes's political philosophy, we need to relate it, on the one hand, to the tradition of political and moral philosophy, and on the other hand, to Hobbes's attempt at the philosophy of nature. As far as the first matter is concerned, Leo Strauss has pointed out that Hobbes founds his criticism of traditional political philosophy on a prior agreement with it. This is about the fact that Hobbes shares the belief of ancient thinkers that political philosophy can be founded on natural law. According to philosophical tradition, "the law is fundamentally distinguished from the pleasant and is by nature preferable to it; or, there is a natural law that is wholly independent of any human compact or convention; or, there is a best political order which is best because it is according to nature."[3] For Hobbes however, human nature is neither political nor social, the "conformity" of the political order with human law is reduced to the necessity of the first, being deduced from the latter by virtue of an anterior principle, namely the necessity of self-preservation for every living being. According to Leo Strauss, Hobbes's conception of human nature is close to that of Epicure, in the sense that it defines the individual good as an accomplishment of that which is agreeable. If man is antisocial, human nature would be defined as the seeking of good in the sensual pleasure, since there is no moral law which stipulates the limitation of actions which give rise to "personal" good, by motivating that they simultaneously harm other people. In order to be grounded, this idea requires a materialistic presupposition, which in Hobbes is the very point of departure for natural philosophy. Strauss calls the two principles "political hedonism"[4], respectively "political atheism": "political atheism and political hedonism belong together. They arose together in the same moment and in the same time,"[5] meaning in modern times. Together they form a "realistic" view of politics, the origin of which undoubtedly lies with Machiavelli. By refusing classical politics and characterizing it as a lack of utility, Machiavelli has replaced the traditional

3 Leo Strauss, *Natural Right and History* (Chicago: The University of Chicago Press, 1965), p. 167.

4 By opposition to Epicure's hedonism which was apolitical. The defining feature of hedonism was identifying good with the agreeable and defining virtue solely as a means of attaining pleasure and of avoiding pain. It is not by chance that modern hedonism, meaning utilitarianism will find, through Jeremy Bentham, a source of inspiration in Hobbes's theory.

5 Strauss, *Natural Right and History*, p. 169.

question "how should man live?" with "how do men actually live?" Abandoning the reflection on a just society and on a good life, the author of the *Prince* has founded "realistic" political philosophy based on a series of observations on the facts which make up the psychological and social universe of men. This means that political philosophy will no longer need to discuss the natural or preternatural foundation of justice.

Hobbes places himself half way between traditional philosophy and Machiavelli, since he accepts the "modern" criticism of the classic utopist politics, yet he does not accept Machiavelli's solution. The difficulty which leads politics, in the *Prince*, is mainly connected to the replacement of moral values with purely political values, derived from political practice, from experience and from the consideration of interests. This is the equivalent of reducing politics to a series of advice of the realistic and cynic wise man towards his prince. Hobbes's interest lies in establishing a political science of universal value, and, as such, he needs to make a concession to traditional philosophy which had known to search for universal, though utopist principles, for a political science. Therefore, the synthesis between Machiavelli and the tradition of classical philosophy implies accepting the "realistic" perspective on the behavior of man and accepts the idea of a natural law, which can allow politics to be grounded in moral principles, without denying "realism".[6] "What Hobbes attempted to do on the basis of Machiavelli's fundamental objection to the Utopian teaching of the tradition, although in opposition to Machiavelli's own solution, was to maintain the idea of natural law but to divorce it from the idea of man's perfection"[7]. The idea is to deduce natural law from the actual behavior of man and to ground moral observation on factual observations. Thus we will see, in the first chapter, the two sources of the Hobbes's reflection on politics: firstly the intellectual tradition of natural law, secondly the political reality of England in his time.

---

6 In this respect, we should mention that a synthesis of Machiavelli and Hobbes was done by the liberal republicanism in England, in the 17th century, in the works of some authors like Marchamont Nedham (*The Case of the Commonwealth*, *The Excellencie of a Free State*), James Harrington (*Oceana*), Henry Neville (*Plato Redivivus: Or, A Dialogue Concerning Government*) and Algernon Sidney (*Discourses Concerning Government*). This authors criticized both Hobbes and Machiavelli and proposed – especially Nedham – a "softened, more Hobbesian Machiavelli – a Machiavelli who puts an emphasis on the people's security" (Vickie B. Sullivan, *Machiavelli, Hobbes, and the Formation of a Liberal Republicanism in England* (Cambridge: Cambridge University Press, 2004), p. 123.

7 Strauss, *Natural Right and History*, p. 180.

1.1 Natural Law and Positive Law: The Classics

The privileged subject for philosophical debate concerning the law was made up by the distinction between natural law and positive law, once the theoretical resources of the opposition between *physis* and *nomos*, as conceptualized by sophists ran dry. The term "law" first appeared in the Greek judiciary vocabulary. Etymologically speaking, it comes from the word "*dikaion*", which in turn comes from "*dike*", a term which initially meant "a way of being" and later on referred to "trial", "human justice". In Latin, the most commonly used term for it is "*jus*"; this would designate the field of action or of maximum pretense which results from the natural definition of an individual or of a group. The word *jus* will later be derived into *justus* and *justitia*. If the people of ancient times had derived *jus* from *justitia*, the people of our modern times will derive *jus* from *jussum* (the one in charge).

In its widest acceptation, the law encompasses all the determinants of freedom. Still, we must note that the significance given to the term was different in ancient thinking and in modern thinking. The people of ancient times understood the law by reference to the division of goods between individuals (private law) and between groups (public law). So, law was either the result of partition, either the instrument by means of which partition was achieved. This refers to the two branches of positive law: private law, reflected in the Civil and Commercial Code, and public law, comprised in the Constitutional Code, the Administrative Code, the Penal Code etc. – the rules of which are set differently in each society, depending on its characteristics. Thus, for Aristotle and St. Thomas Aquinas, law is identified as a righteous distribution of goods and rewards between several individuals and/or social groups. Two consequences should be noted according to the ancient definition: 1) law is inseparable from justice and 2) individual justice is the result of the legal process.

Unlike the ancient meaning of law, its modern sense is based on the idea of power. This can refer to an individual's power over himself and over the environment or to the power of a superior being (human or divine) which produces rules that are imposed over a group of individuals. In the first case, we are talking about *subjective law*, and in the second case, about *objective law*. The main source of the idea concerning the existence of a universal law, a natural law is constituted by morals. The purpose of natural law is to contribute to the attainment of a rational universe and of a universal reasoning. This is why it was stated that all men are rational beings, equals by nature (from this point of view, the person which according to positive law is treated as a slave is equal to a free man according to natural law).

Morally speaking, the laws of any community are valid, as long as they do not contradict this principle. "Human freedom only becomes real if the world is a moral and rational one[8]". Therefore, people need to obey a system of natural laws, laws which are not purely formal and which do not derive from the particular circumstances of some communities or from the will of certain individuals or groups. Such a system of laws would be "inspired by history, but it would be adequate for non-historical circumstances"[9] which require a community's system of positive laws to hold no internal contradictions between different laws and no external contradictions between its laws and the moral principle of the equality of rational beings. If these criteria are not met, people have the natural right of refusing to obey positive law; therefore they obey positive law within the limits of natural law. Natural law only criticizes positive law if the latter does not take into account that people, as rational beings, are equal or if it denies the fact that their defining trait is reason. It does not decide on such matters as, for example, whether one human being can be dominated by another or can become its property; seen that positive law admits this, natural law asks for proof that the being in question is unable to act rationally, and, as a result, it is in need of a guardian, at the same time expecting that in respect to the subdued individual (the slave), the master acts as an educator. Also, natural law does not state that murder is absolutely forbidden, but it states that no one may be killed without proper cause, meaning without proof that the victim is not a rational being and that its existence threatens the rational life of the community.

As for equality among men, we have to mention that natural law does not state that all men are equal as anyone can do anything, but that they are equal assuming that they are all rational and as such, equal as far as positive law is concerned. Positive law does not take into account empirical individuals (which have certain passions, desires and motivations, of an exclusively psychological nature). It concerns itself with rational individuals, as people who fulfill different roles and obligations[10]. Natural law, in its capacity as a critical instance must decide whether if the roles established by positive law are not in conflict and whether the system of positive law does not form an ensemble which contradicts the principle of equality among men, in their capacity as rational beings[11]. Without a content to

8 Eric Weil, *Philosophie politique* (Paris : Vrin, 1996), p. 35.

9 *Ibid.*

10 Therefore, we cannot say that X has rights and obligations, but that X has rights and obligations as a parent, as an owner, etc., who acts rationally and against which a rightful reasonable action if possible.

11 Weil, *Philosophie politique*, p. 37.

which it can be applied (meaning without positive law), natural law is reduced to a form without substance. This content is an historical one since, for example, what is considered to be violent or not depends on the norms of a community at a given time.[12] Therefore, the content of natural law is dependent on the characteristics of the historical communities: their conventions, their morals, their traditions. This, however, does not mean that it loses its validity, merely that it ceases to be a just an idea, and it becomes a practical idea. Therefore, natural law establishes what must be done, in other words, it sets the rules for human behavior. This doesn't just involve the idea of rights, but above all it involves the idea of obligation, since, if man is not under the obligation of doing anything, and his fellow men have no obligation towards him, it means that there can be no rules and no proper conduct. Such obligations are thought to be so obvious, that there is no need to have them stated in writing. Natural law thus becomes a sort of unwritten law, which is superior to written law, because it does not need to be written down in order to be acknowledged. The expression "natural law" has more than one established meaning, of which three are particularly interesting[13]:

1. If we were to look closely at the adjective "natural", then, by natural law we would understand all the rules of human conduct which derive from the nature of things and which therefore are accessible to reason. This is what the widest meaning of the expression is based on, the one that believes natural law to encompasses natural religion, morals, real law and all the rights and duties that man has in relation to his fellow man[14].
2. If we were to think of the term "law" in its philosophical sense, as designating that which relates to duty, by natural law we would understand the specific part of the conduct rules which, by creating a duty for someone, creates a correlative right for someone else. Therefore, natural law is reduced to the ensemble of conduct rules that man must observe in relation to his fellow men.

---

12 Thus, from a certain point in history, slavery is considered unjust and natural law does not permit it, but up to that point, not even the slave spoke out against the institution of slavery, the slave is merely revolted by the fact that he, and not another, has the status of slave.

13 See Th. Jouffroy, *Cours de droit naturel* (Paris: Fayard, 1998), p. 30.

14 There are four types of relations that man has in this world: 1. with God; 2. with himself; 3. with the animate or inanimate objects of creation; 4. with his peers. The first relation engenders natural religion, the second engenders moral, the third engenders actual law and the fourth engenders the actual natural law. Usually, when discussing natural law, we only refer to this last division, since this constitutes its vastest and most complicated part. See Jouffroy, *Cours de droit naturel*, pp. 20–25.

3. In the technical sense of the natural law schools, the narrowest of all, we define as "natural law" only that part of the rules of conduct discovered by reason which are complementary to positive law itself.

However, the specifications of natural law are more diverse if we enrich this analytic panel with the historical meanings which were derived during the evolution of this law concept. Thus, in classical thinking, natural law designated laws which were objectively observed by all peoples (or by most of them), and it is the common origin of any positive law. Therefore, Ulpian and Aquinas distinguish between natural law in its broad sense and natural law in its limited sense. The first is the result of man's generic nature and constitutes the foundations of family law, which is also encountered in animals. In its limited sense, natural law identifies itself with those rights which come from man's specific nature as a rational animal and which are instituted by public reasoning for all peoples.

Modern thinkers of the *natural law school* have spoken of a system of laws which are determined by reason, compulsory and independent of any human will. From this perspective, natural law can be identified with the law in the state of nature, which men need to observe out of interest. In the civil state, positive law must take into consideration the sanctions of natural law. In other words, natural law is the model for positive law, at least as far as its essential components are concerned. Natural law (or the laws of nature) is attributed an universal character, since it is believed that any human being can understand that it represents the perpetual law which cannot be changed the way that positive law is changed. However, this immutability is not without nuances, since natural law is divided by most authors: into *positive* natural law (or prescriptive) and *negative* natural law (or permissive), in Suarez; into *absolute and hypothetical* natural law in Pufendorf; into *primitive and secondary* natural law in Burlamaqui. The first is always compulsory and is immutable (for example, keeping promises), while the second one implies the prior existence of an institution (for example, natural law does not impose the institution of private property, but once private property is established, it enforces its keeping).

During the Age of Enlightenment, philosophers spoke of a universal natural law, which corresponds to the nature of every people; it resides in popular consciousness and it constitutes the initial foundation of elaborate law. By extension, we can consider that positive law is explained through the objective characteristics of a society, which would mean that any law is a natural law. The 20th century registered a return to the idea of universal natural law, seen as an ensemble of permanent finalities (for example: security, justice, usefulness).

In conclusion, we can state that any positive law must have general formal characteristics (equal treatment, the observance of procedures). The diversity of positive laws demonstrates the diversified accomplishment of these universal goals depending on the circumstances, still, without abolishing the idea of natural law. Contrary to natural law, positive law is particular. It depends less on universal justice, since it represents that which is useful to the majority in a community. Another difference between natural and positive law refers to the sanctions they operate with. If the first applies vague or religious sanctions, the latter applies socially organized sanctions. Natural and positive law can be complementary for two reasons. The first one, which modern thinkers emphasize, is that natural law is perceived as a sort of code that positive law must follow and which makes it possible. The latter considers the fact that natural law is incomplete and incapable of establishing by itself the laws of a particular society. In this instance, positive law is thought of as a necessary specification of natural law.

1.1.1 Pagan conceptions

The first expression of the term "natural law" is to be found in ancient Greek philosophy. In the 5th century B.C., Heraclites speaks of a common reasoning which governs the entire universe, as well as of the fact that all common laws are inspired by one single law, namely the divine law. The explicitly formulated concept will only appear in the works of Aristotle, who distinguishes between two types of justice rules, one that is natural and has the same variables everywhere, no matter if the times agree with it or not, and a conventional (legal) one, which is established through the will of men. As far as the existence of the state is concerned, it is considered to be a natural institution, since "a social instinct is implanted in all men by nature" and "he who is unable to live in society, or who has no need of it because he is sufficient for himself, must be either a beast or a God: so, he is no part of a state."[15] It is obvious that, for Aristotle, social life is a requirement for the existence of man and a means of moral betterment, since, by himself, an individual is unable to attain virtue or happiness. The state is a natural institution, which is higher than the family and the individual and constitutes "their substantiality."[16]

---

15 Aristotle, "Politics," in *Complete Works of Aristotle*, vol. 2, edit. Jonathan Barnes (Princeton: Princeton University Press, 1991), 1253a19–1253a39, p. 5.

16 G.W.F. Hegel, *Lectures on the History of Philosophy, Vol. 2: Plato and the Platonists*, translated by E.S. Haldane and Frances H. Simson (Lincoln: University of Nebraska Press, 1995), p. 208.

Referring to this passage from "Politics", W. D. Ross points out that when representing the state as natural "Aristotle does not mean to make it independent of human volition. […] he asserts that it is natural in the sense that it is rooted in the nature of things and not in man's caprice."[17] The Greek philosopher believes that all men living "in nature" have the community instinct, and that "the best of animals" would become the worst of all when separated from law and justice. Therefore, man only exists "as man" in society, justice is a social virtue and law is nothing more than "the principle of order in political society."[18]

As far as equality between men is concerned, it must be said that in Aristotle's philosophy, we do not find an abstract equality between men. Both equality and freedom are dependent on certain concrete conditions. In this context, we can bring up the issue of slavery, which the Greek philosopher believes to be a natural institution. He bases his theory on the assumption that the same relation that exists between the soul and the body (the latter being controlled by the first) must exist between men as well, with some being leaders and others followers. The latter are slaves by nature and for them, it is best to be dominated. Slavery is not a convention: it is rooted in nature, since a lot of men are incapable of ruling themselves and such men should not have any responsibilities or any rights. There is a "profound natural connection" between a master and his slave, but such a connection can become unnatural if the two are only bound by law and violence.

Although Aristotle's contribution was an important one, the first systematic elaboration of the natural law theory is to be found in the thought of *stoic philosophers*. They believed that the entire universe is rationally ordered by the active principle called God, or Universal Reason or Destiny. Each individual nature is part of the cosmos. People are citizens of a divine polis, and they are all commanded by a universal and never changing law. For stoics, virtue means to live in accordance with your own nature and, therefore according to reason (since human reason is a part of divine or universal reason). Since passions and feelings (emotions) are thought to pertain to the irrational part of the soul, the sage will try to free himself from passions and to embrace reasoning as a way of life.[19]

---

17 W. D. Ross, *Aristotle* (London and New York: Routledge, 2005), p. 251.

18 Aristotle, "Politics", 1253a19–1253a39, p. 5.

19 In the modern world, the moral theory of Jean Jacques Rousseau would be considered as a *reprise* of the stoic moral position: "for the impulse of mere appetite is slavery, while obedience to a self-prescribed law is freedom," Rousseau says. Jean Jacques Rousseau, "The Social Contract", in *The Social Contract and The First and Second Discourses*, edited and with an Introduction by Susan Dunn (New Haven and London:

Natural law is discovered by man through the power of his intellect. The idea that there is a natural justice underlain in the essence of man and in his relation to divinity had already been put forth by Plato, but it only became fundamental with the first stoics (Zenon, Chrysipp, Cleanthes), which amplified it and expressed it with great precision. The Romans jurisconsults were influenced by stoic philosophy and they acknowledged the existence of a natural law (*jus naturae*), as being the opposite of civil law (*jus civile* or *jus gentium*).

Acknowledging the existence of natural law also constituted a practical necessity for the roman institutions, as it is known that the Roman Empire included different peoples, with different customs, a fact which called for the acceptance of a universally valid law. Such a law was devised as a system of ideas that pertained to the common traits of all men and represented the very nature of man, at all times and in all places.

The attainment of natural law was disseminated among Romans in the 1st century by Cicero, whose work, *De Legibus* is considered the first treatise concerning natural law. The science of law, Cicero believed, comes from philosophy itself, and philosophy teaches us that all men bear inside them a common reason, which is natural law itself. Speaking of natural law, Cicero states that it is common to all men, it is rational, eternal, it inspires virtue and it protects us from injustice. This law can neither be eluded, nor broken; it cannot be circumvented, neither by magistrates nor by the people, since it is universal, inflexible, and always identical to itself. It cannot be neither denied, nor abolished by other laws since "that law was not thought up by human minds; that it is not some piece of legislation by popular assemblies; but it is something eternal which rules the entire universe through the wisdom of its commands and prohibitions."[20] At the same time, it is not a written law, nor is it taught by others; it is born along with us and it is written in our very nature. It is the source of law, which is identical to reason and, like reason, is divine, invariable, and underlain in nature (not in opinion). It would be absurd to believe that justice is founded on the institutions and laws of men. "If justice – says Cicero – were determined by popular vote or by the decrees of princes or the decisions of judges, then it would be just to commit highway robbery or adultery or to forge wills [...]"[21]. The reason for all that is good is found in oneself and in nature. We do not judge good and evil

---

Yale University Press, 2002), p. 167. The moral autonomy of which Kant speaks must be interpreted in connection with this tradition also, and we must not forget Spinoza!

20 Cicero, "On the Laws", in *On the Commonwealth and On the Laws*, edited by James E. G. Zetzel (Cambridge: Cambridge University Press, 1999), Book II, 8, p. 132.

21 *Cicero,* "On the Laws", Book I, 43, p. 121.

according to the consequences, but according to inherent qualities. The same is valid for virtue, which is merely nature perfected through reason. Thus, above the state there is reason, law, right, and each state is merely a member of a state governed by reason.

The same conception concerning natural law is found in the theory of jurisconsults. Thus, Gaius will assert that the peoples that are led by laws make use, on the one hand, of a law of their own, and on the other hand, o a law which is common for all men. The first one is called *jus civile* (as a specific law of the state), and the second one is called *jus gentium* – the latter is "constituted by natural reason for all [and] are observed by all nations alike."[22] Civil interest cannot conceive natural law, so we can speak of "superior 'naturalness' of the Jus Gentium to the Jus Civile."[23]

Another stoic jurisconsult, Ulpian, will reckon that the principles instituted by universal reason are the following: to live truthfully, to not harm anybody and to give everyone what they deserve. These are also the principles of morals and the universal principles of law.

1.1.2 Christian conceptions

Christianity will deem the stoic doctrine of natural law compatible to its own conception of fraternity between men. An author like Isidor of Seville states that natural law can be observed everywhere, due to the natural instinct that determines us, for example, to get married and to procreate[24]. But those who will give new authority to the idea of natural law will be St. Augustine and St. Tomas Aquinas. They will reconcile it with Christian doctrine and will emphasize its divine character, without mistaking it for divine law. Augustine, for example, believed that, in the true Christian spirit, government is merely a service provided to those governed, and that this was the natural order of things. God wanted man to command animals, but not his fellow man. Unfortunately, the natural

---

22 Gaius, *Gai Institutiones or Institutes of Roman Law,* trans. Edward Poste (Oxford: Clarendon Press, 1904), p. 1.

23 A. H. J. Greenidge, "Historical Introduction" in *Gai Institutiones or Institutes of Roman Law,* by Gaius, translated by Edward Poste (Oxford: Clarendon Press, 1904), p. xxxvi. "The relation between the three types of Jus, known to the theory of Roman jurisprudence, may be expressed by saying that the Jus Civile is the law of man as a member of a state, the Jus Gentium the law of the free man, the Jus Naturale the law of man." Ibid.

24 Cf. P. Janet, *Histoire de la science politique dans ses rapports avec la morale*, vol. 1 (Paris: Alcan, 1887), p. 271.

order has been reversed and, as a result, the yoke of servitude has been placed on the shoulders of the sinner[25]. We note that contrary to the beliefs of Aristotle, Augustine claimed that by virtue of natural law, slavery is unjust. However, it is depicted as a just consequence of sin, and even more so, it has become a natural institution as a result of the corruption of our own nature. Equality between master and slave will only be possible in the city of God; therefore this equality only exists in divine law. Still, the most famous conception about natural law of the time belongs to Tomas Aquinas. His philosophy constitutes an admirable effort to associate two different elements: human and divine philosophy, Aristotelism and Christianism.

Aquinas believed that "law is something pertaining to reason."[26] This is because the law is a rule and a measure of actions, according to which each of us is forced to act or not, but the rule and the measure belong to reason alone. As an act of reason, law is in accordance with the nature of things, since reason can wish for nothing that contradicts nature. Therefore, law is the rule which forces a being to stay within the limits of its nature. According to Aquinas, there are four kinds of law: 1) eternal law; 2) natural law; 3) human law and 4) divine law[27].

Eternal law is the reason behind the governing of things which pre-exist in God, while natural law implies the participation of the eternal reason that carries rational being towards their true purposes. Rational beings receive a sort of participation to the eternal reason, and this participation is the natural right, which can be summed up in a single precept: "good is to be done and pursued, and evil is to be avoided."[28] All the other principles are derived from this fundamental one. Natural law does nothing more than to establish certain common and immutable principles and is completed by a third kind of law, *human law*. The latter is derived from natural law in two ways: a) as the consequence of a principle; b) as a partial determination of an undetermined principle[29]. For example, the "Thou shall not kill" commandment is a consequence of the "to harm no one!" principle, but condemning an actual individual is a determination of the general principle that declares that he who harms another must be punished. In the first case, the law participates to the very strength of the natural law, but in the second case, it only has the strength of human law. Divine law is the one which corrects

25 Ibid. p. 301.
26 Aquinas, Thomas Saint, *Summa theologica* (Christian Classic Ethereal Library), p. 2262.
27 Ibid., II.I, quest. 91, 93, 94, 95 and 98.
28 Ibid., II.I, quest. 94, art. 2, p. 2301.
29 Ibid., II.I, 95, 2.

the imperfections of the natural law and of human law. Four reasons make it necessary: a) it corresponds to man's objective (which is beyond nature) b) judgment passed by men is obscure, while divine law is a clear, accurate and ineffable; c) human law only commands exterior acts; d) human law is unable to punish everything. The inherent purpose of justice is to regulate relations between humans, and its essence is equality.

Aquinas distinguishes between natural and positive law, demonstrating that two things can be equal in two different ways, namely: either through their own nature (according to natural law), either through a contract or joint agreement (in the case of positive law). Also, the same philosopher admits the existence of two levels (degrees) within natural law. The first is present in both humans and animals, and is the result of the absolute nature of things. In a narrow sense, it regards the rights that ensue from man's essential nature as rational animal. Such rights are present through natural reason in all the peoples.[30] At this level, we can distinguish *natural law* from *civil law*. Thus, the first holds all the principles that can be construed from natural law, the principles that constitute integral factors for the existence of society (like trading), while the latter, civil law, concerns itself with the particular laws which any people can adopt, according to its interests.

The biggest issues of natural laws are those concerning property and slavery. Concerning property, Aquinas believes that something can pertain to natural law in two ways: either by virtue of a natural and absolute relation between two things, either by relation to a consequence or to a utility[31]. Thus, if we consider things in themselves, in their essential nature, they are not in the power of man; they are subject to divine power. From this point of view, God is the only owner. If we look at things from the perspective of their usage, we can state that they naturally subject themselves to the power of man, because, by making use of his reason and of his will, man can use the exterior things, provided that they were manmade. Just like Aristotle, Tomas Aquinas asserts private property for three reasons: 1) every man takes better care of the things that belong to him and to him alone; 2) society will be better organized if each of its members is responsible

30 "[…] the rational creature is subject to Divine providence in the most excellent way, in so far as it partakes of a share of providence, by being provident both for itself and for others." Aquinas, *Summa Theologica*, II.I, quest. 91, art. 2, p. 2270.

31 "A thing is said to belong to the natural law in two ways. First, because nature inclines thereto […] Secondly, because nature did not bring in the contrary: thus we might say that for man to be naked is of the natural law, because nature did not give him clothes, but art invented them." Aquinas, *Summa Theologica*, II.I, quest. 94, art. 5, p. 2307.

for what belong to him; 3) there will be peace among men if they are all pleased with themselves and do not covet their neighbors' possessions.

Although private property was not established at the beginnings of natural law, it does not contradict it, as St. Augustine believed also; according to him, in natural law, all is shared among men. Tomas Aquinas introduced another extremely profound distinction in this argument, demonstrating that natural law does not state that all things should be possessed in common, nor does it state that private property should exist. The confusions arise from the fact that Tomas Aquinas does not establish a distinction between possessions, yet nothing points to him being opposed to the idea of property. Obviously, in the nature of things there is no foundation for such a distinction, just like there isn't anything that opposes it, assuming that a human agreement establishes a certain order. Therefore, property is not in contradiction with natural law, it is appended to it through a human invention.[32]

The distinction made by Aquinas is just. The assumed primitive communion of goods is not a positive one, given that all men, by their natural right, must use their goods in common. It is merely a negative communion, meaning that a priori, there is no reason why one man should own something to a greater extent than another.

The second issue concerning natural law is slavery. In respect to this matter, Tomas Aquinas follows along the lines of Aristotle's thinking, mentioning that all he does is to comment on his works. Aristotle believed that servitude among men is natural, as some people are slaves by nature. However, Tomas Aquinas stated, servitude pertains to human law and therefore, the issue at hand is to find out whether equality exists between natural law (*jus naturae*) and human law (*jus gentium*). The Christian philosopher's answer follows a middle path: he admits that there is no natural reason why some men should be more prone to being slaves than others, but he adds that although slavery does not pertain to natural law considered as such, it is still connected to the benefits it brings to both slave and master alike (for what can be more useful for the weak that to be governed and helped by the wiser one?).[33] Thus, although Tomas Aquinas gives

32 "In this sense, 'the possession of all things in common and universal freedom' are said to be of the natural law, because, to wit, the distinction of possessions and slavery were not brought in by nature, but devised by human reason for the benefit of human life. Accordingly the law of nature was not changed in this respect, except by addition." Aquinas, *Summa Theologica*, II.I, quest. 94, art. 5, p. 2307.

33 "But it is evident that the subject as subject, and the slave as slave, are not competent to rule and govern, but rather to be ruled and governed [...] A slave is not capable of

up the principle of natural inequality which made religious equality impossible, he upholds the principle of natural slavery.

Another proof in this respect is constituted by his considerations regarding the state of (natural) innocence. As a result, he will claimed that even in this state, equality is rendered imperfect by the existence of even the smallest natural inequalities, like those of sex, age, knowledge, physical strength, size and beauty, "since in some the reason is perverted by passion, or evil habit, or an evil disposition of nature."[34] The only inequalities that do not occur naturally are those which originate in sin. Still, this raises a question: which are these inequalities born of sin if before sinning people were already unequal due to their souls, their bodies, their ages, their sexes? All of these must have been the inequalities between master and slave, since the existence of inequalities in the state of innocence leads us to believe that the only inequality born of sin is the political one, meaning that between authority and obedience.

Aquinas believed that as far as power is concerned, it can be understood in two ways: either by opposing it to servitude and, in this case, every man who is subjected is the slave (*servus*), either by opposing it to the subject in general – and, in this case, even he who governs over free men can be called a master.[35]

What makes the difference between a slave and a free man is the fact that, while the latter is *causa sui*, the first needs to retrospect to another. Therefore, the master commands his slave since this is in the interest of his usefulness, but this kind of power can only be interpreted as a punishment, which cannot exist in the state of innocence, before a sin has been committed. Unlike this power, political power, held by a free man over other free men could have existed in the absence of sin, meaning that there is only one inequality, namely that between master and slave.

Political power and government pertain to positive right, which originates in natural law, which in turn is merely the image of God's eternal law. Therefore, in this sense, it all comes from God, yet this distant origin of the law does not constitute divine right. This is a special institution, expressly created, by means of which God expressed his particular will. Positive law is connected to the will of men and they have to apply it according to the general and universal principles

taking counsel, in so far as he is a slave (for thus he is the instrument of his master), but he does take counsel in so far as he is a rational animal." Aquinas, *Summa Theologica*, II.II, quest. 47, art. 12, p. 3158.

34 Ibid., II.I, quest. 94, art. 4, p. 2305.

35 Here we can note the similarity to the distinction made by Aristotle between despotic power and legitimate power.

of natural law, but also according to their surroundings, their circumstances and their means. This is also where the diversity of the forms of government originates, as they need to follow nature as closely as possible, meaning that the best form of government is monarchy, since in nature also there is only one supreme power.

One other important contribution for the development of the theory of natural law, which can be classified along with Christian conceptions, is that of Suarez (1548–1617), a Jesuit thinker considered to be the last of the scholastics. His work, *De Legibus,* published posthumously, is a treaty of natural law, according to the principles of medieval philosophy.

By distinguishing natural law from positive law, Suarez believes that the fundamental matter of morals is to demonstrate which is the legitimate foundation of natural law, while the essential matter for politics is to establish the legitimate foundation of positive law (thus, on the one hand, there is the principle of moral obligation, and on the other hand, that of sovereignty).

The foundation of natural law is constituted by "the honesty of actions and rational nature itself"[36]. The acts that follow this nature are good, while the ones that contradict it are bad. Suarez believes that actions are good or bad in themselves, without taking into account any external will or circumstances. Honesty or wickedness do not reside in an action's relation to rational thinking, that which is wrong is not wrong because we judge it as such, we simply judge it as such because it actually is wrong.

We can distinguish two aspects in rational nature: the first points to nature itself as the foundation of human conveniences, and the second to consider the illumination of reason, by means of which he discerns actions which follow natural law from other actions. Considering the first aspect, natural reason is the basis of the honesty of acts, and considering the second aspect, it is law itself. Natural law consists either of the judgment of the spirit, either of the judgment of the legislative, either of the judgment of subjects. In the supreme legislative – God – natural law is one with eternal law. When judging the souls of the subjects, it is the very "light which bears within our soul this eternal law"[37].

Natural law is distinct from conscience, for reason is a rule in general, while conscience is a practical dictate, it is the enforcement of law in particular cases. Its field is far more wide that natural law, since it isn't limited to the mere application of this law, it is also concerned with divine and human law. Another distinction between the two regards the fact that the latter judges past actions

36 Janet, *Histoire de la science politique*, vol. II, p. 56.
37 Ibid., p. 58.

and can be mistaken, while the first judges future actions and virtually excludes the possibility of being wrong.

Concerning natural law, Suarez asks whether it is a prescriptive or an indicative law. It is known that the scholastics made such a distinction between prescriptive and indicative law. The latter indicates what is good and what is bad, while the first establishes that some things should or should not be done. According to the scholastics of the last period (Gabriel, Biel, Almain), natural law only exists as an indicative law that establishes what is right and what is wrong, independent of any will. It is not divine *per se*, since, although it comes from God which is the cause of all things, it does not come from God as a law giver.

The opposite of this opinion is that expressed by Ockam and his school, according to which natural law only resides in the will of God. Any act can be good if God allows it and bad if God condemns it. Natural law, therefore, only consists of divine precepts that God himself can destroy or alter. Something is not god or bad by itself, only divinity decides if it is one or the other.[38]

Halfway between two other extreme opinions, Suarez adopts a balanced view, identical to that of Aquinas: natural law is both indicative and prescriptive, for it indicates what is right and what is wrong, and at the same time it implies the obligation to observe this distinction. It is a true law, a divine law written and given by God, therefore it corresponds to both the nature of things and divine will. Suarez comes to this conclusion, which had already been expressed by his predecessors St. Augustine and Tomas Aquinas.

As far as medieval thinking was concerned, there were two tides of opinion concerning the principle of morals. One of them stated that morals is based on the nature of things; the other asserted that morals was based on divine authority. Some placed the essence of law in intelligence, others in divine will. Both opinions can lead to dangerous consequences: the first opinion is that morals is independent from God and the difference between right and wrong would still exist, even if God did not; the second is that morals is arbitrary, nothing is good or bad in itself and only the order of a superior sets apart good and bad actions.

Caught between the two opinions, Suarez looks for a middle path, hoping to elude these negative consequences. The problem is that even the middle path, according to which the law resides both in the intellect and in divine law, can raise a few objections, because we cannot ask which of these two elements is more important and which is the relation between the two. If the will of God justifies compulsoriness, then this will, can condemn an action which is actually good

38 Here we note that this opinion dates back to antiquity, if we are to consider the contention between Socrates and Eutyphron.

and can allow a bad action, which equals to admitting that moral is arbitrary. If on the contrary, divine will does nothing more than to consecrate compulsoriness, this means that it is pre-existent and it comes from nature itself.

1.2 Natural Law and Natural Right: The Moderns

From the perspective of historical unity and continuity, the theories of natural law present themselves as a series of systems which, despite the diversity of opinions and the fact that they correct each other, develop common issues. No matter the period and the authors that we consider, the theories of natural law showcase a series of constant characteristics found in all authors, namely: 1) Natural right is based on natural law, which is unwritten, unlike positive laws, yet keeps its law status since it commands and enforces the obligations of men, making them capable of just actions and is most often presented as the will of God. 2) It is the expression of reason, the trademark of human nature, making man capable of just action. 3) It constitutes itself as a model or guide, in the sense that it is the expression of a just, eternal and immutable will, the precepts of which are formulated for the greater good. 4) It plays an important role in the state; it is both prior and superior to civil law which is bound to take it into account.

Apart from these characteristics, which are valid for pre-modern theories as well, modern theories of natural law have introduced a series of issues that were unknown to the scholastic philosophers. The most important characteristic of modern theories regards the relation between religion and politics. Although the idea of politics being autonomous from religion is not formulated in the terms of the principle of state's secularity, the matter of division between the power of the Caesar and that of the church could not be ignored after Machiavelli, the Reform and the religious wars. Scholastic thinking was not faced with this issue, except for the dilemma of whether the head of the church, meaning the Pope, can at the same time be the head of secular power. The arguments brought during scholastic contentions were purely theological, although their stake was political. Even when the answer to this question was a negative one, namely that the Pope should only be the head of the church, the separation of politics from religion was not at all indented. Thus, the strongest arguments against politics being engulfed by religion came from the English philosophers and theologians; to prove them right, Henry the 8th, king of England, severed all ties with the Catholic Church and declared himself the head of the Anglican Church.

As for modern theories, they will support the distinction between religion and politics with the aid of some proper philosophical concepts. Thus, in the field of morals a distinction will be made between moral theology and natural law, while in the field of politics the theory of sovereignty is emphasized. The natural rights and obligations of men will be given high importance, thus allowing for the subsequent definition of the civil status and of the conditions under which individuals submit themselves to the authority of the sovereign. As a consequence of this fact, some of the philosophers of natural law will show interest in the relation established between two or more sovereigns. This matter gained particular importance once the confessional diversity of European sovereigns and the diminishment of the role of the church in arbitrating conflicts between sovereigns left external politics without a common judicial principle that all sovereigns could acknowledge. Due to this fact, modern theories concerning natural law are theories of the social contract and implicitly, theories of the laws of peace and war.

The founder of the modern theory of natural law is thought to be the Dutchman Hugo Grotius. He identifies natural law with natural right, representing natural law as a common element to all the peoples and to all men (when considering men individually, putting aside the civil societies of which they are members). Although he admitted the existence of a relevant divine law, Grotius still believed that the basis for international law is constituted entirely by natural law, since the state should not be influenced by religion. In his treatise on natural law, entitled *The Rights of War and Peace*, he considers natural law as being set in human "reasonable nature"[39], as anterior to any convention, as independent from any volitional element, its unique source being the sociable nature of man:[40] "natural law is the rule and dictate of right reason," Grotius says[41].

The immanent law of human reason is, likewise, the rule that sets apart justice from injustice. No human society can ignore natural law, the precepts of which are universal, immutable and compulsory. Just like Aristotle, Hugo Grotius admits that man has a natural penchant for society. Already, from childhood man manifests a natural inclination for pleasing others and for pitying them when

39 Hugo Grotius, *The Rights of War and Peace: Book I*, edited and with an Introduction by Richard Tuck, translated by John Morrice (1715/1738) (Indianapolis: Liberty Fund, 2005) X, p. 151.

40 According to Jean Barbeyrac, the French translator of 1724, whose notes were translated by Morrice in the English edition (1738) and reprinted in the Tuck edition (2005) – here "reasonable" means "sociable": "Our Annotator adds the Words *ac Sociali, & Sociable* in the Text of his *Latin* Edition, because his Author expresses himself in the same Manner […]. He thinks it probable, that the Transcriber or Printer omitted those two Words; and that the Author overlooked the Omission, as he has done in several other Places." Grotius, *The Rights of War and Peace*, p. 151, Note 2.

41 Grotius, *Rights of War and Peace*, p. 150.

they suffer. Reasons adds itself to instinct for the preservation of society, it shows us that actions are honest or dishonest depending on their consequences on rational and social nature. Thus, the foundation of justice and equity is not utility, as the sophists believed, but nature itself which pushes us to trade with our fellow men, even when we don't actually need something from them.

Natural law is its own source and it is "so unalterable, that God himself cannot change it"[42] just like He cannot change the fact that 2 + 2 equals 4. Divinity can only stop that which is bad in itself from being bad (we note that this principle does not belong to Grotius, but to the stoics and to Cicero). Furthermore, even if God did not exist – a hypothesis which was considered absurd – natural law would still be what it is.

Just like Aristotle, Grotius admits that some men are slaves by nature, this status being valid for some peoples as well. The state of nature, in which the possession of all goods was shared, lasted as long as the simplicity and innocence of individuals. As humans proliferated, new needs emerged, their common goods were no longer sufficient and it became impossible for them to live together. As a result, it was convened that each should have the right to possess that which he occupied first (the right of the first occupant) – but this right is not legitimate unless those goods had no previous owner. The most important of goods was considered to be justice, because it brought peace, and the right to war can only be justified in terms of natural law if it is motivated by the preservation instinct: "all Means that we can use for our Preservation are fair and honest."[43]

Hugo Grotius has made two major contributions to the theory of natural law: 1) by defining it as a body of laws that can be discovered through reason, which are still valid, regardless of whether divinity exists or not; through this consideration he sets himself apart from the medieval theories that were influenced by theology, opening a path for the purely rationalistic theories of the 17th and 18th century; 2) by considering that natural law is deductive and independent from all experiences – in the way that mathematicians treat shapes abstractly – the Dutch author tries to analyze natural law independent from any particular fact.

The most influential political theory of the 17th century concerning natural law was that of Thomas Hobbes, which is considered as important for that century as Machiavelli's theory for the 14th and 15th centuries.[44] As we shall see

42 Ibid., p. 155.

43 Ibid., I, chapter 2, III, p. 187. This is, in fact, the thinking of Cicero, which Grotius confirms.

44 By putting Hobbes in the beginning of his course of history of political philosophy, John Rawls has noted that "In my own view and that of many others, Hobbes's

further on, Hobbes thinks of natural law as more of an ideal, in the sense that an organized community's law must fit this archetype, and by so doing it should be in accordance with reason. Therefore, by natural law we understand the rational law, in accordance with the laws of thinking. In this respect, Hobbes declares that there can be no other law of nature than Reason, and reason as well as passions are all part of man's nature. The English philosopher admitted that countries have their specific laws, which need to be observed even if they go against natural laws. The problem at hand is to know where natural law ceases and where positive law starts. But this raises the following questions: how far does the authority of legislative power extend? What should laws be like and to what extent can they interfere with the freedom of the individual?

One important distinction made by Hobbes is that between natural right and natural law. In chapter XIV of the *Leviathan,* he defines natural right as "the liberty each man hath, to use his own power, as he will himself, for the preservation of his own nature; that is to say, of his own life; and consequently, of doing any thing, which in his own judgment, and reason, he shall conceive to be the aptest means thereunto"[45]. And by freedom Hobbes understands "the absence of exterior impediments". Therefore, the difference between right (*jus*) and law (*lex*) is that the first regards the freedom to do or to do not, while the second regards the obligation to do or not to do. By nature each individual is entitled to anything, including to the bodies of other humans. Thus, as long as natural right lives on, there can be no security. This engenders the need for a general rule of reason which states that "that every man, ought to endeavour peace, as far as he has hope of obtaining it; and when he cannot obtain it, that he may seek, and use, all helps, and advantages of war"[46]. The point that needs to be made here is that the first part of this rule renders the first rule of nature, which is to seek peace and to follow it, and the second one renders the sum of the natural rights, which regards defending oneself by any means necessary.

But in order to overcome the state of war, there has to be a power that compels people to obey the same rules in view of common usefulness, meaning that there has to be a state. Natural law and civil law encompass each other. Within the state, natural laws become actual laws. If natural law is part of civil law in

---

Leviathan is the greatest single work of political thought in the English language." John Rawls, *Lectures on the History of Political Philosophy*, edited by Samuel Freeman (Cambridge MA: The Belknap Press of Harvard University Press, 2007), p. 23.

45 Thomas Hobbes, *Leviathan*, edited with an Introduction and Notes by J. C. A. Gaskin (Oxford: Oxford University Press, 1998), chapter XIV, p. 86 [64].

46 Ibid., p. 87 [64].

any organized state, in its turn, civil law is part of natural law "so that the nature of justice, consisteth in keeping of valid covenants: but the validity of covenants begins not but with the constitution of a civil power"[47]. This is to say that there are no significant differences between natural law and civil law, they are merely different aspects of law in general, one of which is written, while the other is unwritten. Still, the right to natural freedom can be restricted by civil laws, as the purpose of making laws is none other than achieving such a restriction that makes peace between men possible, and the law was brought into the world expressly in order to limit the natural freedom of individuals, so that instead or harming one another, they help one another.

Between the doctrine supported by Grotius and Leibniz (the foundation of law on natural right) and that supported by Hobbes (the foundation of law on strength) there is the doctrine of Spinoza, who tries to reconcile the two stands, considering man from both perspectives, that of reason and that of strength. Spinoza's main political works are *The Theological-Political Treatise (1663)* and *The Political Treatise* (which was include in "Posthumous works" in 1677). According to this philosopher, the power which made the existence of natural things possible is that of God. But God possess a sovereign right over all things, and this right is identified with his very power, which is thought to be absolutely beyond all obstacles. This would mean that any natural thing has as much right as it has power, since it is merely a part of God's power, and as such, it participates to the sovereign right of divinity.

Consequently, by natural law we should understand the laws of each individual's nature, which determine his existence and his particular actions. For example, nature gave fish the ability to swim and has made the bigger fish able to eat the smaller fish, and so, according to natural law, all fish swim and the big ones eat the small ones: "and therefore it is by sovereign natural law that fish have possession of the water and that big fish eat small fish."[48] And there is no difference between humans and animals, in this respect.[49]

The first principle of natural law according to Spinoza is the following: *law is equal with power.* Exploited by man, this principle equals the obligation only to

---

47 Ibid., chapter XV, p. 96 [72].

48 Benedict Spinoza, *Theological-Political Treatise*, edited by Jonathan Israel, translated by Michael Silverthorne and Jonathan Israel (Cambridge: Cambridge University Press, 2007), chapter XVI, p. 195.

49 "Here we recognize no difference between human beings and other individual things of nature, nor between those human beings who are endowed with reason and others who do not know true reason." Spinoza, *Theological-Political Treatise*, p. 196.

submit oneself to reason, man's right is measured by the power of reason, but, since nature has made him submit more willingly to passions than to reason, his actual right will not be measured through reason, but through his self-preservation instinct. In the 16th chapter of his *Theological-Political Treatise*, Spinoza says that natural law only forbids that what no one wants and no one is able to do. Everything that to us seems ridiculous, absurd and bad in nature only seems that way because we only see one side of things and because we want to organize nature according to the principles of our own nature. These principles lead to the same conclusions found by Hobbes: in the state of nature, anyone can use everything that he finds useful; therefore everyone holds an equal right over all things, and each person chooses the means through which they pursue their purposes. Also, since all men have the same purpose and are subject to the same passions, they are naturally enemies; "since it is the supreme law of nature that each thing strives to persist in its own state so far as it can"[50], the state of nature is a state of war. But man doesn't just live in accordance with natural law he also lives in accordance with rational law. Through natural law he submits to the general laws of things, and through reason he submits to the laws of his own nature. Reason teaches man that it is useful to live in society, and that peace is better than war and love is better than hatred. Spinoza's outlook is different from Hobbes's because he maintains the existence of natural law even within a state (meaning that the state of war subsists in the civil state, just like in the state of nature). Natural law still exists in the civil state, and all that is missing is the individual's right to take the law into his own hands. But Spinoza diverges from Hobbes especially through the consequences of his doctrine – while the English philosopher, wishes by instructing the state, to have peace proclaimed, the author of the "*Political Treatise*" prefers to have freedom proclaimed. The purpose of the state is to replace natural law with the law of reason, true peace being understood not as a state of servitude, but as a state of agreement.

The first jurist to occupy an academic position, as professor of natural law was Samuel von Pufendorf. In his treatise *De Jure Naturae et Gentium*, he tries to accurately determine the idea of natural law, setting apart natural law from moral theology and the civil laws as follows: natural law is commanded by reason, moral theology is commanded by the holy scriptures, and positive law is derived from legislative power. Pufendorf's great merit is exactly having highlighted the distinction between theology and natural law. This will result in two consequences: the first is that natural law does not extend beyond the limit of

50 Ibid., p. 196.

this lifetime, and the second that it only regulates exterior acts, having the role of making man sociable and of ensuring his earthly happiness. (Natural law treats interior actions only to the extent of their exterior manifestations.)

Pufendorf raises the question of whether natural law exists in the state of innocence, before sin is committed. His answer is an affirmative one, arguing that the principles of natural law are founded on the nature of man and of things, seen how even in his state of nature man has rights and obligations which are universal: "for since man's natural state includes the use of reason we cannot, or should not, separate from it any obligation pointed out thereby"[51]. Still, there are some useless natural laws, namely those that imply an organization of which innocent man had no need (for example, the laws of selling and buying) or those that suit his complete nature (for example, not to lie, not to cheat, basically all of the negative precepts). The theological precept of self-preservation is defined by Pufendorf as man's universal sociability. For him, it is very important to underline the dignity of all men, the greatness of which comes from the initial freedom of the will, which makes all men worthy of respect.

Political authority is not founded in divine law, but in natural law. Natural law comes from the dictates of reason, though this does not mean that any human being is aware of nature's commands. Most men decide what is wrong and what is right by listening to their feelings, but whether their decision is good or bad can only be known after vigorous logical analysis. The best way to establish natural law is to carefully observe the nature of man, his living conditions, his inclinations and his desires. He believes that man's essential characteristics are the self-preservation instinct, the inability to reach his purposes without the collaboration of his fellow man, but also arrogance, irritability and the tendency to destroy.

According to Pufendorf, the fundamental principle of natural law is the following: all that is necessary for the purposes of society must be considered to be required by law. All the statements of natural law are associated with considering the utility of actions. The obligations that natural law imposes regard two types of duties: 1) the absolute ones ("those of every Man towards every Man") meaning humanitarian duties, those that correspond to a person's inherent rights in its present state; 2) the conditional ones ("when the Validity thereof lies upon some Event depending on Chance or the Will of Man") which imply a voluntary

51 Samuel Pufendorf, "On the Law of Nature and of Nations," in *The Political Writings of Samuel Pufendorf*, edit. Craig L. Carr (Oxford: Oxford University Press, 1994), p. 147.

commitment of man towards his fellow man; this kind of duty is the result of conventions and promises[52].

Pufendorf criticizes Aristotle because he considered slavery to be a natural institution, but he also criticizes Hobbes, who based natural law on man's selfishness. However, he considers, in the spirit of Aristotle, that state of nature does not designate a historic reality, because the patriarchal organization of the beginnings of mankind already implied a degree of sociability. What matters to him is that natural independence is characterized by incommodity, because it leaves each individual only his own strength for defense. Thus, civil society is presented as a salutary institution, one that is established on the basis of social contract.

When speaking of the thinkers of the 17th century that were concerned with natural law we must not forget G.W. Leibniz, a philosopher who, without having expressly discussed natural law, still has some diffuse ideas in his jurisprudence works. Leibniz criticizes Pufendorf concerning the three aspects of his theory on natural law, more exactly concerning his purpose, his object and his efficient cause. As far as purpose is concerned, he reproaches him having limited natural law to the limits of this existence. He believes this means to mutilate a science and to repress numerous duties, making natural law present in atheists as well. Concerning the object, the limitation of natural law to exterior acts means to identify good with exterior acts, to such an extent that people who are corrupt on the inside can be considered good as long as they appear to be innocent on the outside.

Pufendorf is wrong – Leibniz believed – in respect to the efficient cause of law. "He, does not find it in the nature of things and in the precepts of right reason which conform to it, which emanate from the divine understanding, but in the command of a superior."[53] According to him, this action is compulsory, consistent with the latter law, and it is defined as the decree by which the superior forces the subject to comply with the actions set forth by his will.

According to Leibniz, God is the universal sovereign, he is the grace behind all the treatises and he supports justice, but in a certain sense, he is subject to an obligation, being subject to the rules of wisdom, reason and.[54] The observation that

52 Samuel Pufendorf, *The Whole Duty of Man According to the Law of Nature*, trans. Andrew Tooke (1691), edited with an Introduction by Ian Hunter and David Saunders (Indianapolis: Liberty Fund, 2003), pp. 95, 118.

53 G.W. Leibniz, "Opinion on the Principles of Pufendorf (1706)." In *Leibniz's Political Writings*, edit. Patrick Riley (Cambridge: Cambridge University Press, 1988), p. 70.

54 See Christopher L. Johns, *The Science of Right in Leibniz's Practical Philosophy* (New York: Bloomsbury, 2013), p. 19.

needs to be made here is that Leibniz, like the ancient philosophers, is tempted to identify morals with natural law (Kant will be the one who will try to separate the two sciences again). He will identify three stages within natural law: 1) the stage of strict law; 2) the stage of equity; 3) the stage of piousness. Each of these has a higher degree of perfection than the previous one. *Strict law* is defined as the law of peace and war, seen how, between two people, the natural law is that of peace, as long as none of the two attacks the other. But between a person and a thing (which is defined by the lack of intelligence) there is a permanent law of war (for example, a lion may kill a man and the other way around). A person's victory over a thing is called possession and it is identified to the state of captivity of the latter. But if we attack a person, be it in respect to its own being or in respect to its possessions, we grant this person the right to war, meaning the same right that we hold over things. *Equity* or *equality* consists of the existence of a harmonious proportion between two or more people. It is the one which determines us not to kill a person who wrongs us, but to seek arbitration and most of all, not to do onto others what we do not want others to do to us. Equity is the one that prompts us to obey strict justice. *Superior authority,* the third principle of justice can be given by nature of by convention. By the nature of things, God alone is superior and man subjects himself to his authority through piousness. The essence of this kind of justice is expressed by Ulpian's maxim *honeste vivere.*[55]

In the preface to the initial treatise *De Codice Juris Gentium Diplomatica Monitor*[56], Leibniz defines natural law as a "moral power", while necessity is a "moral necessity". Moral power is the one that, in a righteous man, balances natural power, and by "a righteous man" we mean a man who loves all others to the extent that reason allows him to do so. What can be held against Leibniz is the fact that, in his vision, we can easily confuse law and morals, this being an aspect that Pufendorf had tried to avoid. His merit consists in that, unlike Pufendorf and Hobbes, he established the fact that natural law does not originate in any kind of power, not even in divine power, it is simply grounded in God's reason and in the very nature of things.

Without a doubt, the most important modern philosopher of natural right is John Locke. His main work, *Two Treatises on Civil Government,* constitutes, together with Hobbes's *Leviathan* the milestone writings of political philosophy of the 17th century. Following Hobbes's example, who was the first modern thinker

---

55 The three degrees of natural law are the "three precepts of right" of which speaks Ulpian: "to live honestly, to harm no one, to give to each his own." Johns, *Science of Right in Leibniz,* p. 26.

56 Janet, *Histoire de la science politique*, vol. II, p. 249.

to try and find the origin of civil society in a certain previous state of nature, Locke departs from the same hypothesis and tries to justify it in another way. Concerning how long men were in their state of nature, Locke answers that this stage lasted until the formation of common political society. Therefore, states which are independent from one another are in their state of nature as long as there are no other laws that regulate the relations between them, apart from natural law or from the law of the strongest. Even as allies, sovereign states preserve their state of nature among themselves as long as there isn't a certain convention between them, one which would put an end to the state of nature. For example, a Swede and an Indian were to meet in the forests of the Americas and were they to conclude some conventions between them, this would not make them a political society. Such conventions must be, without a doubt, respected, for truth and faith are natural obligations, and they "belongs to men as men, and not as members of society"[57]. Therefore, the state of nature is the relation that exists between men by virtue of their human nature, notwithstanding the relations of civil society. In this sense, the state of nature will always exist, since before being citizens of a civil society, men are just that, men. The state of nature is not a state a savagery, it is a state in which, in the absence of civil and political laws, a law still exists and this is the natural law. This natural law precedes and is superior to all civil laws; it is above individual passions and obligations, for all men.

The law of nature makes itself known through nature, but Locke does not make it clear how this comes to be, whether it is innate or acquired, and in the latter case, whether this acquirement takes place gradually or immediately through the use of intellect. In their state of nature men do not kill, they do not harm each other, they keep their promises and they respect those that they come into contact with. Therefore, even if in this state the individual is free, he still has duties towards others, which result from his observance of natural law. Thus, according to Locke, unlike what Hobbes stated, the state of nature is a state of peace, with the mention that he uses this concept in more of a rational and moral sense than in a historical one. He places equality at the origin, but this is more an equality of right than one of fact, since he is referring to equality in terms of morals, of the identification of faculties and needs. Unfortunately, the state of nature is difficult to preserve, as men aren't always rational, and the order it establishes is troubled by passions. Violent people claim all the goods for themselves, threatening the

57 John Locke, *Two Treatises of Government*, edited with an introduction and notes by Peter Laslett (Cambridge: Cambridge University Press, 1988), p. 277. [Second Treatise, II, 14].

property, the freedom and even the lives of others. It is only now that state of nature turns into a state of war, precisely because men no longer obey natural law. In this state of war, natural law entitles each man to defend himself and to punish those who wrong him[58]. Thus, any individual is entitled to punish he who defies natural law, and who by so doing places himself in the position of enemy of humanity. Since in their state of nature all men are free and equal, it results that there is no such thing as the natural domination of one man over the other. Moreover, man's first duty is to preserve his own life, no one has any right over his own life and even more so, cannot attribute onto others this right that de does not poses. No one can pass onto another his natural freedom, the only warranty for his conservation. Still, Locke[59] admits one exception to this principle, namely power over a criminal or over a war prisoner. In such cases, he acknowledges the master's absolute power, beyond any convention. However, this concession is "imprudent, since this right of war is what jurisprudents ground slavery on."[60]

In conclusion, we can state that according to the reasoning of Locke, in their state of nature, men are free and equal, they have duties one towards the other, they are united in a family for which power is determined through obligations and submission and is limited by law, the natural right of property exists and it is grounded in work, there is a natural power to punish those who perpetrate injustice, as no man has the right to dominate another.

1.3 Civil war and sovereignty in England

The theories presented above are all *modern* theories of natural law. The purpose of presenting them chronologically was to demonstrate that there has been an intellectual progress as far as they are concerned. The distinction that needs to be made is between English and continental theories of natural law: Hobbes and Locke, on the one hand, and all the other philosophers of natural law on the other. Thus, we can note that the continental theories of natural law are closer to scholastic philosophy. In such theories, human nature is defined only as being rational, and sociability as being written in man's nature. This is why the central idea of moral philosophy is the subjection of passions and the triumph of reason, which is to say that political theory is focused on the idea of the moral obligation that an individual has towards society. According to this tradition, "the fundamental moral fact" was given by the obligation that any man has towards

58 Ibid., pp. 278–279. [Second Treatise, III, 18].
59 Ibid., p. 272. [Second Treatise, II, 8].
60 Janet, *Histoire de la science politique*, vol. II, p. 208.

society, given that society is seen as prior to the individual and as a source of humanity. It was the individual's duty to contribute to the perfection of the state through moral perfection, aiming to gain virtue and to bring his contribution to the common good. In return, society would contribute to the individual's perfection, in view of achieving its natural purpose. An isolated individual was considered to be "insufficient", which made him less than human or inhuman, precisely because of the inability to morally perfect himself within society and to contribute through his moral life to the accomplishment of the natural outcome. The strict relationship between moral and politics in traditional philosophy refers therefore to the prescription of some obligations that each individual must observe in order to contribute, through his personal life, to the common good. Plato, Aristotle and St. Thomas Aquinas were interested in how the definition of the justice of the city and of common good could be formulated. They insisted on the connection between the justice of the individual and the justice of the city and every time they reached the troublesome issue of government. The classical question in political theory "What is the best kind of government?" started from the supposition that a certain form of government was better than all the others, regardless of the form preferred by each philosopher. This meant that state policy was seen as strictly dependent on the political man's ability to accomplish the ideal of wisdom and prudence, of moral moderation and of virtue.

None of this issue is present in the works of Hobbes or Locke: they believe that the individual is prior to society, and this belief leads to the idea that the man has no *natural* obligation towards society or towards the sovereign, he only has *natural* rights – we are referring to those rights which every human being has by virtue of its humanity and that he can never relinquish. We will show just how Hobbes explains the institution of civil society starting from the state of nature and from the violence of passions. On the one hand, the moral and political theory of English philosophers can be seen as a consequence of their empiricist doctrines in the theory of knowledge.[61] On the other hand, this empirical theory

---

61 However, it is not obvious that Hobbes was an empiricist. He is that kind of philosopher who is rationalist among empiricists, and empiricist among rationalists. As A.P. Martinich has noted, "He is an empiricist in the sense that he maintains that all terms of the substantive terms of a proposition must be traceable to sensation. He is rationalist in the sense that he maintains that all scientific knowledge is necessary. He is not am empiricist if that means maintaining that scientific propositions are statements of empirical fact. And he is not a rationalist if that means maintaining that some scientific propositions are nonanalytic." A.P. Martinich, *Hobbes: A Biography*, (Cambridge: Cambridge University Press, 1999), pp. 131–132.

itself can be seen as a social and historical foundation; the empiricist theory of knowledge would serve precisely to ground a certain morals and a certain politics.[62] From this perspective, the reason of the *coupure épistémologique* must be bound to the importance of England's political events of 17th century for the construction of a new political philosophy. For this reason, a look over the historical and political situation of 17th century English society seems relevant.

At the beginning of the 17th century, the British monarchy was one of the oldest and best organized European monarchies. However, this fact did not stop England from falling prey to one of the most violent civil wars. As a matter of fact, English history in the 17th century was marked by two major events: the civil war of 1640–1649 and the Glorious revolution of 1688. In 1625, Carol the First is crowned king of England. Since he took over the throne, he followed a drastic taxation policy, just like his predecessor, James the First. In 1688, the Parliament decided to remind the king that he was bound to follow the laws of his kingdom. For this purpose, the famous *Bill of rights* was drafted, as a statement of what were thought to be the principles of the *Magna Carta*[63]. "The original feature of the *Bill of rights* lay in the fact that it sought to fix definite bounds between the royal power and the power of the law."[64] Although he hesitates, the king accepts the Bill which becomes one of the fundamental laws of the kingdom, though not for long. Although he had accepted, the Parliament refuses to grant Charles I the *Tonnage and Paundage* tax[65]. Even more so, in 1629, the

62 "The antirationalistic approach, which regards man not as a highly rational and intelligent but as a very irrational and fallible being, whose individual errors are corrected only in the course of a social process, and which aims at making the best of a very imperfect material, is probably the most characteristic feature of English individualism." F. A. Hayek, *Individualism and Economic Order* (Chicago: The University of Chicago Press, 1984), p. 9.

63 The *Magna Carta*, written in 1215, stipulates in general terms that the king must uphold the laws of the state and the rights of his subjects. If he breaks them, he is no longer owed loyalty and the subjects have the right to rebel. In time, the *Magna Carta* will become the "charter of British freedoms", and each king, up to the 15th century, would have to swear, on more than one occasion during his reign to observe this text. During the reign of the Tudors, this book will be ignored, and will only become a counterweight of divine right during the reign of James I.

64 André Maurois, *A History of England*, translated by Hamish Miles (London: Jonathan Cape, 1937) p. 281.

65 That is fixed taxes on wool and leather trading which the Parliament used to vote for as a means of income for the king.

"Three Resolutions"[66] were adopted, which were intended to prevent the dissolution of the Parliament by the king. The king will arrest at the end of the session 9 members of the House of Commons and will dissolve the Parliament.

Between 1629 and 1640, there was no Parliament in England and a series of political and religious conflicts took place, with fierce repressions against the puritans. The culmination was the attempt to impose upon the Scotts, who were fierce about defending their Presbyterian church, the Anglican rite, which caused a strong resistance from the Scotts, one which Charles I wanted to crush with the force of arms. Therefore, in 1640 Charles I is forced to summon the Parliament. Far from being supportive of the war with Scotland, the House of Commons demands retribution for the damages it had suffered. John Pym, a rebel ex-parliament member in 1629, the head of the opposition in Parliament starting with 1640, rememorizes all of Charles's mistakes and the Parliament negotiates with the Scotts. After a session of only 18 days, the Parliament was once more dissolved by the king. Since he had no money, no loyal soldiers and he had been defeated by the Scotts, the king had to accept the will of his subjects and to summon a new Parliament, which will be known in history as the Long Parliament. This one, which was dominated by puritans, imposes parliamentary control over the royal government. A Catholic uprising started in Ireland and the arrest of John Pym led to the first confrontations between the king's troops and those of Parliament. At the start of the civil war, none of the partisans of Parliament wanted the king to be removed. No one imagined that he could be disposed of. The Parliament just wanted to have control over the king. Essex, the general in charge of the Parliament's forces, recommended his troops to be cautious, since "the King, even if beaten, would still be king, whereas they, if beaten, would merely be rebels or traitors"[67]. This is the obvious proof that the idea that the king is sacred was still intact at that time.

At the time when civil war broke out, the parliament's side benefited from the support of the better developed regions of South East England, especially that of the strong economic centre of London. On the other hand, the royalists had a well-organized army, which earned them a few victories, though, no decisive ones. Gradually, the Parliament also managed to develop its military forces. Oliver Cromwell played the key part, representing the new nobility. Possessing

---

66 These define as an enemy of the state: 1) anyone who tried to introduce papism to England; 2) anyone who would try to levy taxes that Parliament had not sanctioned; 3) any merchant or other person who would try to pay such taxes that hadn't been sanctioned by Parliament. See Maurois, *A History of England*, p. 283.

67 Maurois, *A History of England*, p. 298.

remarkable military and political abilities, he would become the Revolution's most prominent figure. Cromwell, a puritan, was obsessed with the idea of creating a model army, and so he recruited the *Ironsides*, which were renowned for the strict discipline of their soldiers. Following the example of this detachment, he created the army of the "new model", which proved its worth in the battle of Naseby (1645). This was the defining moment for the Parliament's victory, although the fighting went on until 1648, when, in the battle of Preston, the troops of the Parliament, led by Oliver Cromwell defeated the Scottish troops which supported the king. The latter is arrested and will later be executed[68], in 1649. After the king's execution, Oliver Cromwell assumed the political power, he dissolved the Long Parliament and become the self-proclaimed Lord Protector in 1653, as he did not wish to take on the title of king, which would have been a serious inconvenience for a man who had become popular precisely for having fought against royalty. In turn, the new regime was called a Protectorate. The prerogatives of the head of state were particularly broad, surpassing those of the monarchs of continental Europe. Cromwell used these to keep down any and all protests. To break the opposition, he transformed the Protectorate into a puritan military dictatorship, which will last until his death, in 1658. His son, Richard, will succeed him, but he will be forced to abdicate, as he proved to be unable to resolve the latent conflict between the army and civil power. The Stuart monarchy was restored in 1660 when Charles II took the throne. The Parliament instituted in 1660 does not dear to limit the king's power in any manner by means of a constitutional law. As a result, the abuses will be soon felt, since the king went as far as to dissolve Parliament in 1681. After the Restoration, the first nucleus of political parties, the *tory*[69] and the *whig*[70], started to emerge in England. While the first favored royalty and supported land ownership and the Anglican Church, the latter were dissidents and London merchants. The dissolution of Parliament was followed by a period of persecution against the Whigs. Their leader, the

68 In *Behemoth*, Hobbes describes him as "a man that wanted no virtue, either of body or mind, nor endeavoured anything more than to discharge his duty towards God, in the well governing of his subjects". Thomas Hobbes, "Behemoth, the history of the causes of the civil war of England", in *The English Work of Thomas Hobbes of Malmesbury*, collected and published by Sir William Molesworth, vol. VI (London: John Bohn, 1840), p. 166.

69 *Tory* (*toryes*) was the name given to Irish brigands by their opponents, and it insinuated that they were nothing more than Catholics in disguise.

70 This is an abbreviation of the word *whigamores* which designates groups of puritan peasants from the west of Scotland. They were given this name by the *toryes*.

count of Shaftsbury was forced to exile himself in Holland, where he died, while other important militants of his party found their death in jail or on the scaffold. England had been overtaken by "a wave of mystical devotion to royalty"[71]. This is also the time when the work *Patriarcha* of Sir Robert Filmer was published posthumously, in which he claims that, since the king is the successor of the patriarchs and the father of his subjects, any rebellion against the king is a patricide. Charles II dies in 1685, and the throne of England will be taken by James II (James VII of Scotland), who, as a Catholic, intends to restore Catholicism in England. The civil and military offices were occupied by catholic clerks and officers, and they went as far as arresting the bishop of Canterbury. However, the English people remained patient as long as the king had no male heir, and the heiress to the throne was Princess Mary, protestant, the wife of the Duke William of Orange. But, in 1688, Mary of Modena, the king's second wife (a Catholic), gave birth to a son, which caused the people to riot. When William of Orange disembarked in Western England, enjoying the support of aristocracy and of the army alike, James II leaves London in disguise and hides in France. In February 1689, William of Orange is crowned king under the name of William III. It was obvious that after this coronation there could be no more talk about the divine right of the kings of England. The disposal of the Stuarts and the institution of a new monarchy, a constitutional one, is known in the history of England as The Glorious Revolution. William III ratifies the *Declaration of Rights*, which became later *The Bill of Rights* and established the rights and the duties of the people and of the king. Government was based on the separation of powers. Political leadership was divided between the king, the Cabinet and the Parliament. The important political theories tried to justify from a theoretic point of view the events of those troubled times. These were the theories of Thomas Hobbes and of John Locke. The first focused on the civil war, while the latter chose the Glorious Revolution. While Locke considered the events of 1688 to be the triumph of freedom and of reason, Hobbes was horrified by the events of 1640, and this feeling will define his political philosophy and will establish its main goal, that of searching for the conditions which allow an individual to be defended through violence, especially through the kind of violence engendered by a civil war.

This short presentation is sufficient to show why there is an essential difference between the English political theories (those of Hobbes and Locke) and other modern theories of natural law. Leo Strauss uses the expression "natural public law" in order to distinguish between the political philosophies of Hobbes and

---

71 Maurois, *A History of England*, p. 330.

Locke and the natural law school of thought (represented by Grotius and Pufendorf). This author points out that, while Machiavelli have introduced in politics the subordination of all interests to the "reason of state", Hobbes and Locke get the credit for pointing out that the only legitimate "reason of state" consists of insuring the rights and safety of the individual: "The 'rational state' school replaced 'the best regime' by 'efficient government'. The 'natural public law' school replaces 'the best regime' by 'legitimate government.'"[72] In other words, the theories concerning "natural public laws" are searching for a social order which will be legitimate in any circumstances. The idea of the best form of government is abandoned and replaced with the idea of a just order of things, which will have to offer a universal solution for the political problems. This solution will be seen in a strict connection with the issue of political obligation and of its relation to moral obligation. The reversal of the report of antecedence between the individual and society leads, in political philosophy, to the possibility of conceiving the idea of a state which could bring order "even for a nation of devils (if only they possess understanding)", as Kant will put it[73].

In this respect, we believe that the difference between Hobbes and Locke should be treated with the proper interest when discussing the matter of *which legitimate form of government is suited to human nature?* It is important to analyze the direction of these differences, since the relation between political thinking and moral philosophy is being constantly redefined, and implicitly, so is the issue of human nature. Analyzing the differences between the political theories of Hobbes and Locke might lead to answering the question whether political philosophy systems are developments of a scientific conception of man, or to the contrary, whether theories concerning the nature of man are mere artifices, meant to justify one doctrine or another. The debates concerning the political theories of Hobbes and Locke are all the more significant since the two theories are no longer the expression of a new political thinking, but that of a new conception concerning man – a conception which at the time was qualified as scientific. Apart from this, there is the prejudice according to which, since the definitions given to human nature by Hobbes and by Locke were formulated in the spirit of Britain's 17th century, the differences between the two philosophers

72 Leo Strauss, *Natural Right and History* (Chicago: The University of Chicago Press, 1965), p. 191.

73 Immanuel Kant, "Toward Perpetual Peace: A Philosophical Sketch", in *Toward Perpetual Peace and Other Writings on Politics, Peace, and History*, by Immanuel Kant, edited and with an Introduction by Pauline Kleingeld, translated by David L. Colclasure (New Haven and London: Yale University Press, 2006), p. 90 [Ak 8:366].

have a "local color", so there is nothing more to learn from them. The success of these theories would be owed to the global expansion of the Anglo-Saxon civilization or to that of European civilization in general, and they are nothing more than the expression of liberal ideology, which means that it would be pointless to discuss, for example, about the issue of human rights in the Islamic world or in other countries in which liberalism and democracy have not made their way. Through such arguments, the critics of liberalism claim to take into account the diversity of cultures and the existence of a type of man whose "nature" has been culturally shaped, so it is impossible to apply to him the liberal theory of human nature without submitting him to an act of violence.

Far from admitting that the political theories of Hobbes and of Locke are ahistorical, we believe that setting them in the context of the liberal culture of the 17th century England does not make them any less universal. Therefore, the first common teaching of all thinkers in the tradition of "natural public law" refers to the idea that there is a human nature and that, despite the pressure exerted by cultural, social and political factors, it is immutable, at least as long as we think of the human being as a person. Therefore, there can be no absolute denial of the thesis that the human being has a set of natural rights and that society needs to ensure that such rights are granted, unless we deny that man is actually a person. Although some cultures which deny the individual's definition as a person do exist, this is not a sufficient reason to say that the people of that cultures are less human or that they have fewer rights. Speaking from the point of view of the relation which man, as a person, has with his fellow men, there are only two possible conceptions concerning human nature: either as sociable (Locke, Rousseau), either as non-sociable (Hobbes). To think of man as a person implies thinking that he is an individual and a person outside the social rules imposed through an agreement or through force (positive laws); therefore, the idea of human nature – of man as a person – logically leads to the hypothesis of a state of nature. Next, we shall see how the concepts of "human nature", of "state of nature" and of "social contact" have lead, in Hobbes's political theory, to the consolidation of the idea that the precedence of the individual over society meant that the purpose of the civil state is the individual himself.

Chapter 2: The theory of sovereignty

According to Hobbes (*Elements of Philosophy*), philosophy deals either with natural bodies (*De corpore*, 1656), in which case it is natural philosophy, either with artificial bodies, in which case it is civil philosophy (*De Homine*, 1658, *De Cive*, 1642). In the study of natural bodies, Hobbes was influenced by the physics of Descartes, which dominated the European thought at that time. Concerning the study of artificial bodies, like states and communities, the Cartesian method requires the consideration of the "elements" of these bodies, which are human individuals with their instincts, passions and reasons. If the science is science of constitutive causes, as Aristotle have pointed out in the age of the Greeks, in the time of mechanistic science this universal condition requires to explain how the various parts and elements are put together and work mechanically as a whole. With respect to civil bodies, this methodological standpoint requires to consider the elements as if they were free and independent or, in other words, as if there would not be composite bodies which are called "commonwealths". Thus the hypothesis of the state of nature and its moral correlate – the doctrine about the natural laws – follow from a methodological assumption. It is for this reason that Hobbes put together the new Cartesian methodology and the old reflection on natural law initiated by the Stoics and the Roman jurists; however, this old reflection has been already reformulated by the school of natural law, so that Hobbes retake the modern version of this doctrine.

2.1 The human condition of mankind

As we have pointed out above, by "natural law", *jus gentium* or *jus naturae*, Hobbes's contemporaries understood a law which was valid for all, as it had been conceived by Roman jurists who had given it a practical and precise content: as a system of ideas corresponding to the common traits of all the people and peoples of the Roman empire, one that represented the very nature of man throughout the ages. Hobbes goes even further in this direction; he accepts the natural law more than an ideal law, meaning that, if the law of an organized community should correspond to this archetype, it must also represent an agreement with reason. In *De corpore politico*, Hobbes says that here can be no other law than reason, and reason, just like passions, is part of human nature. The term of "nature" is interpreted by the English philosopher as *ultima ratio*, indicating that which is natural, necessary and general. Thus, by "natural law" he mainly understands a "rational law", one that is in perfect agreement with the laws of thinking.

Therefore, in order to discover the natural law ant to show how the knowledge of natural law is possible, a description of human nature must be done.

2.1.1 The two postulates of human nature

In this respect, Hobbes's theory of human nature could be summed up by presenting the "two most certain postulates of human nature"[74], namely that of "natural appetite" (*cupiditas naturalis*) and that of "natural reason" (*rationis naturalis*).[75] By virtue of "natural appetite", man wishes to possess by himself all the goods that nature has intended for common use. This appetite originates in sensibility, in animal nature. Essentially, human appetite is not different from animal appetite; all that separates the two is man's ability to use reason. For that matter, reason is the only faculty that sets man apart from the animals and, thanks to it, man is less of a slave to sensitive and fleeting impressions and is, therefore, able to anticipate future actions and needs. This is the reason why his appetites do not pertain to the immediate present, but to the future. As a result, man becomes the strongest, the most feared, the wisest and the most dangerous of animals. The desires of men are infinite, they "attain to more riches, honours, or other power; so their appetite continually groweth more and more; and when they are come to the utmost degree of one kind of power, they pursue some other, as long as in any kind they think themselves behind any other."[76] Felicity is therefore "a continual progress of the desire, from one object to another."[77] Furthermore, humanity's inclination consists of a "perpetual and restless desire of power after

---

74 Strauss, *Natural Right and History*, p. 8. In the English translation of *De Cive*, from 1651, reprinted in the Oxford edition by Howard Warender, the phrase *duo certissima naturae humanae postulate* is translated by "two maximes of humane Nature." Thomas Hobbes, *De cive: The English Version* (Oxford: Oxford University Press, 1983), p. 27. Richard Tuck, in his new edition (with a new translation by M. Silverthorne), considers that "There are many mistranslations or misunderstandings of Hobbes's text" in this edition. See Richard Tuck, "The translation" in *On the Citizen* by Thomas Hobbes (Cambridge: Cambridge University Press, 1998), xxxvi. Silverthorne translation is: "two absolutely certain postulates of human nature" (Hobbes, *On the Citizen*, p. 6).

75 For the explication of this postulates, see also Johann Sommerville, "Lofty Science and Local Politics", in The *Cambridge Companion to Thomas Hobbes*, edited by Tom Sorell (Cambridge: Cambridge University Press, 1996), pp. 246–247.

76 Thomas Hobbes, *The Elements of Law Natural and Politic*: *Part. I*: *Human Nature* (New York: Oxford University Press, 1994), chapter VII, § 7, p. 45.

77 Hobbes, *Leviathan*, edited by J.C.A. Gaskin (Oxford: Oxford University Press, 1998), chapter XI, 1, p. 65 [47].

power, that ceaseth only in death."[78] This conception concerning human appetite corresponds with Hobbes's intention in political philosophy, of demonstrating that man spontaneously and continuously desires more and more power.

Aspiration towards power can be of two types: rational or irrational. It's just that the latter, which is a lot more frequent than the first, can be interpreted as man's natural appetite. Rational aspiration implies the rational determination of power; since it is not prior to exterior motivations, to experience and to education, it cannot be considered natural, meaning innate. In the 13th chapter of the *Leviathan*, given this distinction, Hobbes demonstrates that the growth of power for self-defense is necessary, as long as men continue to desire to dominate one another, irrationally. The latter rationally have the right to defend themselves, and in so doing to use force, and therefore power. This demonstrates that rational aspiration is finite and allowed. As natural appetite, irrational aspiration originates in vanity. As far as means in which natural appetite manifests, passions are nothing more than particular means of aspiring to domination and of acknowledging it, which equals vanity.

Starting from Hobbes's conception on human nature, one might think that, according to him, man is evil by nature. Leo Strauss sums up this erroneous interpretation as follows: "if this conception about natural appetite is just, if man does find in his nature the pleasure of triumphing over others, than man is evil by nature."[79] Strauss points out that Hobbes himself refused this consequence and that it is solely for this reason that, when enumerating at the end of the *Leviathan* the causes which lead to the war of every one against every one, he granted vanity last place.

For this purpose, in the *Preface* of *De Cive*, he notes that although malice is a passion of our soul with which we are born (given by nature), this doesn't means that men are naturally evil, since malice is nothing else but the lack of reason; or the use of reason comes with age and education and it is not given by nature, So men possess by nature passions as fear, anger, desire, but this doesn't mean that nature is the cause of malice. Since man, by his nature, is an animal, we shouldn't think of human malice as anything but similar to the innocent malice of animals, which makes it unintentional. By placing vanity last, Hobbes aims to "put 'vanity' more and more into the background in favour of innocent competition, innocent striving after power, innocent animal appetite, because the definition

78 Ibid., chapter XI, 1, p. 66 [47].

79 Leo Strauss, *The Political Philosophy of Hobbes: Its Basis and Its Genesis,* translated by Elsa M. Sinclair (Chicago and London: *The University of Chicago Press*, 1963), p. 13.

of man's natural appetite in terms of vanity is intended as a moral judgement and consequently man cannot be considered an innocent animal anymore."[80]

The second principle of Hobbes's theory on human nature is that of the existence of a "natural reason". This reason determines men to avoid violent death as much as possible, which is thought of as the greatest evil in nature. Therefore, self-preservation is a consequence of the existence of natural reason. The preservation of live is the *sine qua non* condition for satisfying any appetite, making it the *first good*, as it is stated in *De Homine*[81]. It is noteworthy that Hobbes preferred the negative expression "avoiding death" to the positive one, as "preservation of life". The motive goes without saying. Reason is the one which shows us that the "first good" is the preservation of life. In exchange, the fact that death is the greatest evil is revealed to us through passion, and this passion is the fear of dying. Man would not be inclined to think of the preservation of life as the first good, if he is not forced to do so by "that terrible enemy of nature, death."[82] Therefore, it is "from death and pain" that man preserves his life, which is "not against reason", says Hobbes in the same place. A second reason, strictly related to the first and which pleads for the use of the negative expression takes into account the fact that, according to Hobbes, the preservation of life is the first good, without also being the supreme good. It is a means of attaining the greatest good of all, happiness (or felicity), which is understood as "continual delight, consisteth not in having prospered, but in prospering"[83] or, as Hobbes says in the definition of *voluntary motions* (the passions): "continual success in obtaining those things which a man from time to time desireth, that is to say, continual prospering [is that men call *felicity*]."[84] As a matter of fact, a supreme good, the kind which brings peace to one's spirit, does not exist.

On the other hand, death is the first, if not the greatest evil, supreme evil. Although each person desires what he thinks is good for him, his first concern is to avoid "what is evill, but chiefly the chiefest of naturall evills, which is Death."[85] Death is the denial of every good, it constitutes a sole absolute reference by reference to which man can organize his life. Thus, while there are no true limits

---

80 Ibid., p. 14.

81 "Moreover, the greatest of goods for each is his own preservation." Hobbes, *Man and Citizen* (De Homine *and* De Cive), edit. Bernard Gert, trans. Charles T. Wood (Indianapolis: Hacket Publishing Company, 1991), p. 48.

82 Hobbes, *Elements of Law*, I, chapter XIV, § 6, p. 79.

83 Ibid., I, chapter VII, § 7, p. 45.

84 Hobbes, *Leviathan*, chapter VI, 58, p. 41 [29].

85 Hobbes, *De Cive*, chapter I, § 7, p. 47.

in the order of good, the first good being different of the greatest good, when it comes to evil, there is a common identity between the first evil, the greatest evil and supreme evil. It is only in relation to this evil that we can limit our desire. Therefore, Hobbes is perfectly justified to use the negative expression "avoiding death", and not the positive expression "preserving life", since "we fear death infinitely more than we desire life."[86]

The ultimate evil is not death in itself, but the violent and painful death, "that terrible enemy of nature [...] from whom we expect both the loss of all power, and also the greatest of bodily pains in the losing."[87] Men threatened by other men are likely victims for violent deaths. The rational awareness of death is not the greatest evil, but the fear of death is, meaning the passionate and indomitable abhorrence of death. This is the foundation of natural law since "by the word Right is [...] signified [...] that liberty which every man hath to make use of his naturall faculties according to right reason: Therefore the first foundation of naturall Right is this, that every man as much as in him lies endeavour to protect his life and members."[88] At the same time, fear of death is at the core of every civil society, since "the Originall of all great, and lasting Societies, consisted not in the mutuall good will men had towards each other, but in the mutuall fear they had of each other."[89] By this fear Hobbes understands the foresight of a future evil which give birth to suspicion, distrust, and precaution. In one word, there is fear in men's every action, even in the most courageous ones since sometimes the strongest armies negotiate for peace fearing from each other's power. It is not the rational principle of self-preservation, but this fear of a violent death which constitutes the root of any right and of any morals.

The opposition which serves as a starting point for Hobbes's political philosophy is that between vanity as a source of natural appetite, on the one hand, and the fear of a violent death, as passion which leads man towards reason, on the other hand. Since Hobbes reduces man's natural appetite to vanity, he has no choice but to identify the principle of morality in the fear of a violent death and not in the aspiration towards self-preservation. This is because man's natural appetite originates in vanity, meaning that man strives, by nature, to determine other people to acknowledge his superiority, his purpose being to draw pleasure from this. This does not mean that he naturally wants the whole world to step aside and to bow down to him. Happiness means to always surpass one's

86 Strauss, *The Political Philosophy of Hobbes*, p. 16.
87 Hobbes, *Elements of Law,* I, chapter XIV, § 6, p. 79.
88 Hobbes, *De Cive*, chapter I, § 7, p. 47.
89 Ibid., chapter I, § 2, p. 44.

competitors. Human life can be compared with a race in which "we must suppose to have no other goal, nor no other garland, but being foremost."[90]

Having experienced danger, man dedicates himself to reason, since "men have no other means to acknowledge their own darkness, but only by reasoning from the unforeseen mischances, that befall them in their ways."[91] This self-knowing is accomplished through the unanticipated representation of supreme evil – death. Thus, the requirement for self-knowing is constituted by the threat of an unforeseen death. In order to understand the reason that determined Thomas Hobbes to establish the origin of morals in the fear of a violent death, we must first understand why and how man (whose natural passion is vanity) experiences this. A vain man, who thinks of himself as superior to others, cannot convince himself that self-esteem is justified unless his superiority is acknowledged by others. The greatest pleasure of man is to consider the others like inferiors to him and to act consequently toward them, fact that generates resentments and will of revenge. Or, in order to take revenge, the offended party aims to take the life of a person to which he has now become indifferent. All the hatred signs which are shown to each other lead to conflicts and battles in such a degree that men may consider finally that life itself is useless. Without going to great lengths to preserve his own life, man can no longer wish for the other to stay alive. Although, since there can be no triumph over death, the aim of revenge is not death but the subjection of the enemy.

Therefore, the goal of the arisen conflict is not to get the other person killed, but to submit it. Still, we must not lose sight of the fact that this is a conflict in terms of a real up-close struggle. At some point, a real offence and physical pain engender the fear of losing our life. This fear tempers rage, it makes the feeling of contempt relative and it turns the will for revenge into hatred, so that there is a mutation concerning one's objectives, since "to kill is the aim of them that hate, to rid themselves of fear"[92]. The struggle for dominance turns into a fight to the death. Faced with the threat of death, natural man is forced to know the supreme evil when he is forced to bring about someone's death in order to preserve his life. By killing his enemy, he only escapes to the threat of death temporarily, since every man is his enemy and another will make him face the same peril. In order to protect his own life, not just momentarily, but in the long run, man needs companions. There are two ways in which men can come together, "either by constraint, or by consent; By Constraint, when after fight the Conqueror makes

90 Hobbes, *Elements of Law,* I, chapter IX, § 21, p. 59.
91 Hobbes, *Leviathan*, chapter XLIV, 2, p. 404 [334].
92 Hobbes, *Elements of Law*, I, chapter 9, § 6, p. 52.

the conquered serve him either through feare of death, or by laying fetters on him: By consent, when men enter into society to helpe each other, both parties consenting without any constraint."[93] The first way is closer to the desires of natural man than the latter, since it embodies the path between killing one's enemy and agreeing with him. The fear for his own life in battle tempers or even eliminates the desire for triumph and makes the individual submit to his enemy, provided that his life is spared. For that matter, the enemy has attained his purpose, meaning the recognition of his superiority, and cannot take his opponent's life without losing his honor, "for nothing but fear can justify the taking away of another's life."[94] Thus, the relation between master and slave is born. The winner who has preserved his honor becomes the master. The loser, who obeys out of fear of dying, recognizes his weakness, and by so doing he loses his honor and becomes a slave[95]. The dominance of the master over the slave is similar to another type of dominance, called *patriarchal dominance,* both of which are characteristic of the state of nature and are built upon the despotic reign which is the state of nature.

2.1.2 The war of every one against every one

Like most philosophers of natural law, Tomas Hobbes makes a distinction between the state of nature and the civil state, the latter being instituted once a social contract is concluded. In Hobbes, the state of nature is a logical, not an historical hypothesis. It is a consequence drawn by inference from the empirical description of human passions and of people's lifestyle in the absence of a sovereign power to compel them. The state of nature and the social contract are not put forward by Hobbes in order to establish the historical origins of states. He was aware that, despite any resemblances with the state of savage tribes in America, the state of nature was never real and most of sovereign states origins were the conquest. The aim of social contract theory was to determine people of imperfect sovereign states to accept that they have a complete obligation toward a sovereign and so to create a perfect sovereign state. For this purpose people must act as if they would leave the state of nature due to the social contract.[96] The

---

93 Hobbes, *De Cive*, chapter I, § 14, p. 50.

94 Hobbes, *Elements of Law I*, chapter 19, § 2.

95 See Hobbes, *Elements of Law*, II, chapter XXII, § 2, pp. 126–127; Hobbes, *De Cive*, chapter VIII, § 1, pp. 117–118; Hobbes, *Leviathan*, chapter 20, p. 132–133 [102].

96 See C. B. Macpherson, *The political Theory of Possessive Individualism Hobbes to Locke* (London: Oxford University Press, 1964), p. 20.

fundamental idea of contractualism[97] is that, by nature, all men are equal, both in their physical and their spiritual faculties. In this respect, Hobbes points out that those who do not accept this equality base their assertions on a "vain conceit of one's own wisdom, which almost all men think they have in a greater degree, than the vulgar; that is, than all men but themselves, and a few others, whom by fame, or for concurring with themselves, they approve."[98] However, Hobbes also believed that since men have such a hard time admitting that others are wiser than them, this rather makes for an argument in favor of their equality, than one in favor of their inequality, given that there is no clearer proof of the equal distribution of things than the fact that each is content with his share.

This equality of faculties resides in equal hope of attaining one's own goals. The two types of equality (that of faculties and that of the hope of attaining one's own goals) also bring about an equality of rights. The equality of faculties is proven through observation and experience. The equality of faculties should not be understood in absolute terms, in the sense that every individual has the same capacity; it is merely proven by the fact that the weak can easily kill the strong, which implies a moral equality[99]. This matter is presented by Hobbes in all three of his works on political philosophy as follows:

1) In *Elements of Law*: "[…] if we consider how little odds there is of strength or knowledge between men of mature age, and with how great facility he that is the weaker in strength or in wit, or in both, may utterly destroy the power of the stronger; since there needeth but little force to the taking away of a man's

97 In the recent philosophical debates about the contract theory, there is a distinction between contractarianism and contractualism. The former is rooted in Hobbes and is based on the idea of mutual self-interest and of maximization of self-interests in a bargain with others (in our time David Gauthier being its most important advocate), while the latter has its roots in Kant, being grounded on the idea of moral equality of persons and on the respect of their autonomy (John Rawls and Thomas Scanlon being the most relevant authors). Apart the different arguments and nuances concerning this matter, the distinction is fundamentally "concerned with what reasons and forms of reasoning are justifiable." Elizabeth Ashford and Tim Mulgan, "Contractualism", in *Stanford Encyclopedia of Philosophy* (2012), in paragraph 1 ("What is contractualism?"). It means that individuals are "taken to be motivated by self-interest" or by a "commitment to publicly justify the standards of morality to which each will be held." (Ann Cudd, "Contractarianism", in *The Stanford Encyclopedia of Philosophy*, 2013).

98 Hobbes, *Leviathan*, chapter XIII, 2, p. 82 [61].

99 Macpherson, *The political Theory of Possessive Individualism*, p. 74.

life; we may conclude that men considered in mere nature, ought to admit amongst themselves equality."[100]

2) In *De cive*: "For 1'f we look on men fullgrown, and consider how brittle the frame of our humane body is, [...] and how easie a matter it is, even for the weakest man to kill the strongest, there is no reason why any man trusting to his own strength should conceive himself made by nature above others: they are equalls who can doe equall things one against the other; but they who can do the greatest things, (namely kill) can doe equall things. All men therefore among themselves are by nature equall."[101]
3) In *Leviathan*: "Nature hath made men so equal, in the faculties of the body, and mind; as that though there be found one man sometimes manifestly stronger in body, or of quicker mind than another; yet when all is reckoned together, the difference between man, and man, is not so considerable, as that one man can thereupon claim to himself any benefit, to which another may not pretend, as well as he. For (...) the weakest has strength enough to kill the strongest, either by secret machination, or by confederacy with others, that are in the same danger with himself."[102]

Each of the presented versions includes a principle of right or of obligation, one derived from the observation of the state of affairs. The arguments above demonstrate[103] that men *need* to admit that they are all equals (*Elements*), that there is no reason why one should think about himself to be superior to others (*De Cive*), and that no one can claim to have a moral authority over other men (*The Leviathan*). Hobbes defends the natural equality of rights, derived from *de facto*

100 Hobbes, *Elements of Law,* I, chapter XIV, § 2, p. 78.

101 Hobbes, *De Cive*, chapter I, § 3, p. 45.

102 Hobbes, *Leviathan*, chapter XIII, 1, p. 82 [60].

103 With regard to the Hobbesian politics and ethics, the word "demonstration" must be understood in the sense of scientific demonstration, as it is pointed out by Hobbes himself in *De Homine*: "Finally, politics and ethics (that is the sciences of just and unjust, of equity and inequity) can be demonstrated a priori; because we ourselves make the principles – that is, the causes of justice (namely laws and covenants)- whereby it is known what justice and equity, and their opposites injustice and inequity, are." Hobbes, *Man and Citizen*, p. 42. According to David Gauthier, this passage is essential for understanding that, in Hobbes, "demonstration rests on construction", as in geometry, since "the method is rather to begin from definitions that set out the generation of the civil commonwealth, and demonstrate a priori the characteristics of its members." David Gauthier, "Hobbes on Demonstration and Construction," *Journal of the History of Philosophy*, 35(1997): p. 510, 516.

equality, thinking that this is so obvious, that it no longer requires a demonstration. There is no reason why one should think about himself as being superior to his fellows, since equality is a manifest fact.

The second kind of equality, that of the hope of attaining the desired purposes, is presented in the *Leviathan* as a consequence of the first type of equality. On the other hand, in *Elements* and in *De Cive*, this equality is derived from the fact that men equally wish to preserve their life. As a result, the possibility of the normative and moral equality of men is involved in the real equality of natural individuals.[104] As in the case of equal faculties, Hobbes designates as natural rights those consequences of the natural needs of men which are not absurd, nor blamable; there would be rights as long as would be desires which men [would?] tend to satisfy. Equality is therefore understood as a natural right. Additionally, natural right is an initial given which sanctifies the freedom that any man possesses that of acting as he sees fit, according to his judgment and to his reason, in order to preserve his own life.[105]

In the *Leviathan*, the issue of equality is found on two major levels: 1) the combatants' equal impossibility of hoping to obtain superiority (dominance) without taking too many risks and 2) the equal fear present in all individuals that they might lose their live if they drop their guard even for a second. The relations between man and his peers are defined by mutual and universal fear. "The cause

104 "And forasmuch as necessity of nature maketh men to will and desire *bonum sibi*, that which is good for themselves, and to avoid that which is hurtful; but most of all that terrible enemy of nature, death, from whom we expect both the loss of all power, and also the greatest of bodily pains in the losing; it is not against reason that a man doth all he can to preserve his own body and limbs, both from death and pain. And that which is not against reason, men call RIGHT, or jus, or blameless liberty of using our own natural power and ability. It is therefore a right of nature: that every man may preserve his own life and limbs, with all the power he hath." Hobbes, *Elements of Law I*, chapter XIV, § 6, p. 79. "[…] for every man is desirous of what is good for him, and shuns what is evill, but chiefly the chiefest of naturall evills, which is Death (…) It is therefore neither absurd, nor reprehensible; neither against the dictates of true reason for a man to use all his endeavours to preserve and defend his Body, and the Members thereof from death and sorrowes; but that which is not contrary to right reason, that all men account to be done justly, and with right. Neither by the word Right is any thing else signified, then that liberty which every man hath to make use of his naturall faculties according to right reason." Hobbes, *De Cive*, chapter I, § 7, p. 47.

105 See Anne-Laure Angoulvent, *Hobbes et la morale politique* (Paris: Presses Universitaires de France, 1994), p. 30.

of mutuall fear consists partly in the naturall equality of men, partly in their mutuall will of hurting."[106] Each time men crave the same thing, they become enemies. So war is a natural phenomenon, it is set in the anarchy of passions and in this sense it is opposed to the social order. The equality of all men and the perpetual war are the main characteristics of the state of nature. On the one hand, equality is given by mutual and universal fear; on the other hand, it is given by every one's right to all things. It is obvious that war is the first consequence of the natural equality of men, and this war is of every man against every man (*bellum omnium contra omnes*). There follows that peace is nothing else than the recognition of inequality among men. In the state of peace, that is civil society, equality is preserved only as formal dependence of citizens on the same rules, the citizens being the subjects who obey the only sovereign.

A peculiar distinction which is implicitly made in *Leviathan*[107] is that between the natural condition of mankind and the state of nature. By "natural condition of mankind" it is understood the *general condition* of humans in which, by virtue of their nature, they find themselves or tend to find themselves in all sorts of circumstances, having passions and purposes which are more or less in accordance with the right reason, within or outside the society or. In other words, the human nature is the same in all the individuals and, in this respect, there is no difference between the tribes living in America and the aristocracy of England. On the other hand, by "state of nature" it is understood the *particular situation* of men when there is no common power, as well as the situation which follows after the dissolution of common power. Moreover, in *The Leviathan*, Hobbes rarely makes use of the expression "state of nature", as he prefers using such expressions as "natural condition of mankind" and "state of war". By "natural condition of mankind" it is understood that the behavior of men, which is essentially determined by their violent passions, can not only be presumed in the so called "state of nature", but also be observed in the situation of modern people who live from time to time under the pressure of extreme circumstances, like civil war. In *De Cive* there is no such a distinction, as Hobbes chooses to use the expression "state of nature" for describing both the (general) condition and the (particular) situation. Therefore, the natural condition is itself identified with the state of war, and we can assert that, in this work, Hobbes sometimes understand the state of nature in a more historical sense.[108] The concept of state of nature in Hobbes tends

106 Hobbes, *De Cive*, chapter I, § 3, p. 45.
107 Hobbes, *Leviathan*, chapter XIII, pp. 82–86 [60–63].
108 Macpherson, *The Political Theory of Possessive Individualism*, p. 28.

to explain two separate circumstances: that of antipathy and that of competition, in which men find themselves as a result of their own nature and of the extreme circumstances of war.

When Hobbes identifies the three sources of conflict in the nature of man, namely: competition over winnings, distrust for personal safety and glory for reputation,[109] he intend to say that these three causes of conflicts can be found in any society, but they become destructive only when there is no sovereign power to keep them under control. These are the natural inclinations of man in the state of society[110]. War doesn't just consist of the act of fighting, "but in the known disposition thereto, during all the time there is no assurance to the contrary."[111] Therefore, according to Hobbes, war can be defined as the strategic confrontation which makes any man to destroy or to dominate his peer, so that the latter may not accomplish his desires.[112] As in the state of war there is no law, there is no such thing as justice or injustice. Strength and trickery become the fundamental virtues. Hobbes rejects the Aristotelian idea according to which justice and injustice are faculties of the soul, since, if this was the case, they would also be present in an isolated individual. These qualities can only be found in the institutional schemes of civil society.[113] The description of the state of nature follows a terrifying pattern: the land is no cultivated, there is no navigation, nor any spacious constructions, nor arts, and the greatest evils are the constant fear and the threat of a violent death. In the Hobbesian outline of the individual psychology, two aspects are to be highlighted: 1) by their nature, men are selfish creatures,[114]

---

109 Hobbes, *Leviathan*, chapter XIII, 7, p. 83 (62].

110 The concept of "natural" in Hobbes is not opposed to the concept of "social" or of "civil", these being natural dispositions found in the civilized man as well as in the natural man.

111 Hobbes, *Leviathan*, chapter XIII, 8, p. 84 [62].

112 "Each tries through physical force to compel the other to do his will", Carl von Clausewitz, *On War* (Princeton: Princeton University Press, 1989), p. 75. But "in war many different roads can lead to the goal, to the attainment of the political object, fighting is the only possible means." Ibid., p. 98.

113 The idea of institutional schemes in the discussion about justice is from John Rawls who speaks of "the arrangement of major social institutions into one scheme of co-operation", this one "must not [being] confused … with the principles which apply to individuals and their actions in particular circumstances", John Rawls, *A Theory of Justice* (Cambridge: The Belknap Press of Harvard University Press, 1999), p. 47.

114 In his *Introduction* to Leviathan, Michael Oakeshott makes much clear this idea, by saying that the egoism of natural man is not a moral defect: "neither moral, nor a defect; it is only the individuality of a creature shut up, without hope of immediate

whose actions are intended to obtain and to secure the good for themselves, and to avoid the evil; 2) death is the supreme evil. As far as man's life is concerned, it is described as "solitary, poor, nasty, brutish, and short."[115] The same presentation of the state of nature is to be found in *De Cive*, where Hobbes describes men as "few, fierce, short-lived, poor, nasty, and destroy'd of all that Pleasure, and Beauty of life, which Peace and Society are wont to bring with them."[116]

As Hobbes grounds his doctrine on the assumption of the state of nature as a state of war, he tries to demonstrate the existence of this state by means of reasonable arguments. Firstly, he makes sure to overturn the Aristotelian principle according to which man is a social animal. This does not mean that man is unfit for society, since it is obvious that he finds solitude unbearable and he is able to make conventions.[117] But this natural inclination can explain only some accidental reunions; it does not explain as well the state of civil society based on social contract and political conventions. Upon further examination, we will see that man is not sociable by nature, but by accident. If a man loves humanity in another human being (as being human), then he should love all human beings equally. In society, men only search for their own well-being, be it that of the flesh or that of the spirit (namely, a good self-opinion and superiority over others). They are all inclined by nature, not towards sociability, but towards domination and, as a result, towards war. A confirmation of the fact that man's natural tendency is to seek destruction comes from observing the behavior of civilized man as follows: when leaving on a journey, every man arms himself and tries to be accompanied,

---

release, within the world of his own imagination." Michael Oakeshott, "Introduction to *Leviathan*" in *Hobbes on Civil Association*, by Michael Oakeshott (Indianapolis: Liberty Fund, 1975), p. 63.

115 Hobbes, *Leviathan*, chapter XIII, 9, p. 84 [62].

116 Hobbes, *De Cive*, chapter I, XIII, p. 49.

117 There are some interpretations of Hobbes which point out that his political theory is fundamentally related to the patriarchalist thought of the 17th century. Especially his model of family would be grounded on the hypothesis about the "sexual contract", as shown by Carole Pateman ("God Hath Ordained to Man a Helper: Hobbes, Patriarchy and Conjugal Right", *British Journal of Political Science*, 19(1989): p. 459). According to Corneliu Bilba, this interpretation seems to be a good argument against the classic Hobbesian studies, since it acknowledges the existence of conventions which precede the political contract, like family. "An undeniable proof for this interpretation is that civil order does not contest paternal domination within family and this is because the natural relations within family are not a state of war" Corneliu Bilba, "The Parent-Child Relation in Hobbes: Beyond Private Life and Public Reason", *Research and Social Intervention*, 32 (2011): p. 177.

and when he sleeps, he closes the doors, he even locks his coffers in his own home, and these are all things that could not be explained, if there were not the state of nature as a state of war.

Therefore, the natural condition of which Hobbes speaks is not an historic event, one that can be described as been occurred in a certain moment in time (although Hobbes invokes the situation of primitive tribes in America). His doctrine is not grounded on a political anthropology (*avant la lettre*), but it is rooted in the "inexorable result of the objective data of human psychology."[118]

Another logical consequence of the natural equality of men and of the state of war is the fact that, before the institution of civil society, there was no property, no governance, every man possessed what he could obtain and only for a little while. If man's greatest good consists in his self-preservation, his greatest evil being the perpetual fear of death, and if the state of nature means living in danger and fear, it follows that leaving this state and finding a way to obtain peace and security is an absolute necessity.

2.2 Natural laws as moral percepts

Overcoming the state of nature implies the concentrated effort of passions and of reason. The passions which drive men towards peace are the fear of death, the desire for well-being, but also the desire for sensual pleasure (since virtues are born out of the personal interests related to pleasure, although the love of virtue comes from the love of praise). As far as reason is concerned, it suggests those articles of peace which are called "natural laws," and it constitutes the rational foundation of civil states.

"The concept of a law of nature is perhaps the most difficult of Hobbes's fundamental moral terms to explicate."[119] Hobbes distinguishes between natural

118 E. Socaciu, *Filosofia politică a lui Thomas Hobbes* (Iaşi: Editura Polirom, 2001), p. 226 [my translation]. However, there are authors who think that the natural condition is "based on a general and multivalent view of human nature": "some elements of Hobbes's description [...] can be traced back to early anthropological accounts of the Americans", other elements can be found in classical tradition of poetry, rhetoric and philosophy, and there is also the "game-theoretical model of the prisoner's dilemma." Kinch Hoekstra, "Hobbes on the Natural Condition of Mankind", in *The Cambridge Companion to Hobbes's 'Leviathan'*, edited by Patricia Springborg (Cambridge: Cambridge University Press, 2007), pp. 117, 114, 113.

119 David Gauthier, *The Logic of Leviathan: the Moral and Political Theory of Thomas Hobbes* (Oxford: Clarendon Press, 1969), p. 35.

right and natural law. In this meaning, nature's right is each man's freedom to use his own power in order to preserve his own life, as his own reason and judgment dictate. By freedom, the English philosopher understands "the absence of external impediments: which impediments, may oft take away part of a man's power to do what he would; but cannot hinder him from using the power left him, according as his judgment, and reason shall dictate to him."[120] Natural law is a precept or a general rule which is discovered through reason and which stops an action that could destroy one's own life or which could endanger the means of keeping one's life. At the same time, it does not permit to overlook an action by which life would be better preserved. Natural right refers to the freedom of doing or of not doing something. The laws of nature are common for all of mankind. Each man was given by nature a right over all things, including over the bodies of other men. This means that as long as natural right over each thing persists, there can be no security.

2.2.1 The seeking of peace and the transfer of right

This brings us to the next general rule of reason: "that every man, ought to endeavour peace, as far as he has hope of obtaining it; and when he cannot obtain it, that he may seek, and use, all helps, and advantages of war."[121] The first part of this rule comprises the first law of nature, which is that of *seeking peace and following it*, while the second part comprises the sum of nature's rights, which is self-defense, by any available means. Concerning the first law, we can say that while passions drive man to obtain what he wishes (which could generate conflicts with others), reason advises him to renounce the state of war and to insure his self-preservation through association and through mutual understanding. Still, there is no contradiction between passions and reason, given that both have the same goal, namely self-preservation, it is just that the first acts against its own purpose, while the second re-established that purpose.

It follows that passion is not legitimate, and if the individual were strong enough to always fulfill his wishes, then he wouldn't need any other rules; if he would always be the victor, he wouldn't have to seek peace, and if he could always be the master, for him, natural law and natural right would be the same thing. Or, given that men are all equal, such a security is impossible; this makes war the greatest evil for everybody and peace the greatest good.

---

120 Hobbes, *Leviathan*, chapter XIV, 2, p. 86 [64].

121 Ibid., chapter XIV, 4, p. 87 [64].

The second law of nature is derived from the first, according to which someone agrees, at the same time as others and to the extent that this is necessary for peace and for his own defense, ***to give up his right*** over all things and to be content with "so much liberty against other men, as he would allow other men against himself."[122] This requirement which needs to be met in order to obtain peace is expressed in the Gospel: "do onto others as you want done onto you" and it is that law which is common to all men: "do as you would be done by". As long as each individual preserves his right to do as he pleases, the state of war is maintained. This does not mean that all rights can be remised; thus no one can give up his right to put up a fight when threatened. The purpose of renouncing one's rights is personal safety and, for that reason, no right which goes against this purpose can be conceded.[123] A right may be conceded either by renunciation, either by transfer. He who gives up a right is not concerned with he who will benefit from that right, as long as the renunciation implies conceding the said right for the benefit of one or more individuals. Both cases result in the obligation, for the one who has renounced or transferred a right, to not oppose the benefits which ensue from the said right for the one who has conceded it. It is his duty not to annul the act that he has willingly undertaken, and as a result, any opposition would equal an injustice towards authority.

The transfer is voluntary, since the author seeks to obtain a personal benefit, the concession of some rights is undertaken in exchange of some advantages, namely in exchange of personal safety. The mutual transfer of a right between two or more people is called a *contract*, while the promise of conceding a right is called a *pact* or a convention. If the transfer is not mutual and only one party concedes its right, in the hope of gaining the friendship or the help of the one who benefits from the transfer, or even in the hope of a heavenly reward, then it is neither contract nor pact, but a *gift* or a charity.

The signs of a contract are either explicit, either implicit; in the first case, the discussion is either in the past or in the present tense, while in the latter future tense is used, so in this instance we are dealing with promises. These do not lead to obligations, because they are merely expressions of the desire to transfer a right which belongs to the person in question. Hobbes believes that there is a significant difference concerning the tense used when expressing a promise

122 Ibid., chapter XIV, 5, p. 87 [64].

123 "It is understandably easy to misconceive the role of Hobbes's second law of nature. Confusing what the law does with what it requires us to do, one then supposes that the law does impose restrictions on the right of nature." Gauthier, *The Logic of Leviathan*, p. 54.

(if it is past or present tense, for example "I have given, or do give to be delivered to-morrow")[124] then renouncing the right in question is a clear matter. Also, statements such as "I will that this be thine to-morrow" and "I will give it thee to-morrow"[125] have different significances. In the first case, we are dealing with an act of the present will, while in the other we are dealing with the promise of an act of the future will. Therefore, in the first statement a future right is transferred, while in the second one nothing is transferred.

In the case of contracts, the right is transferred no matter what tense is used, since any contract is a transfer or a mutual exchange of rights. The contract is designating as the fulfillment of a promise, and nonobservance of a contract equals losing ones honor. Pacts based on mutual trust can be violated and are made in the state of nature, meaning when there is no higher power over the two parties that people could fear. Once the state of war begins, there are no more conventions, nor pacts. However, when a higher power does coerce the parties, such conventions or pacts cannot become void since in these circumstances, human passions are surpassed by the authority and by the power it possesses. The contractor believes that the object of the pact can be achieved, therefore the promise of an impossible action cannot be the object of a pact; still, if that which was thought possible turns out to be impossible, this does not make the pact void. One can be free from a pact either by honoring it, either by retransferring the right on which the obligation is grounded. Thus, it is understood why pacts which are made out of fear are valid. (For example, the promise made to a thief, when he is threatening to kill us, must be kept, since if this were not the case, it would mean that we could break any promise, at any given time, which would mean that even civil laws would not be compulsory.) Hobbes adds, however, that such pacts can be annulled by civil law.

However, there are some limitations concerning the obligations undertaken through a pact. Thus, none can forsake their right to defend themselves or the right to live, this being a law of nature. Therefore, the promise of nonresistance to force, in a convention, does not imply the transference of any right, nor does it bind the individual. Hobbes admits that, if a convention such as "*unless I do so, or so, kill me*" might be possible, in return, a convention such as "*unless I do so, or so, I will not resist you, when you come to kill me*"[126] is impossible. Human nature made it so that man will always choose the lesser evil; in the given situation, the

---

124 Hobbes, *Leviathan*, chapter XIV, 15, p. 90 [67].
125 Ibid., chapter XIV, 15, p. 90 [67].
126 Ibid., chapter XIV, 29, p. 93 [70] [Hobbes's italics].

threat of dying while resisting is the lesser evil, compared to a certain death with no resistance. Also, a convention becomes void if an individual is forced to accuse himself. Accusations from family members are also invalid, just like those obtained through torture. Before the constitution of society, there was nothing which could strengthen an established peace convention, other than the fear of God. Therefore, all that to individuals in the state of nature could do was to ask one another to swear with God as their witness. However, swearing doesn't make the obligation comprised in a pact any more binding, since if the pact is legitimate, it binds one in front of God, with or without an oath, and if it is illegitimate, it doesn't bind the parties at all, even if it is sealed by oath. By an oath, Hobbes understands "*form of speech, added to a promise; by which he that promiseth, signifieth, that unless he perform, he renounceth the mercy of his God, or calleth to him for vengeance on himself.*"[127] We could say that the second law of nature is the one which forces us to mutually transfer our rights, which insures peace for mankind.

2.2.2 Justice, gratitude and other natural laws

From the second law ensues a new one, which binds men to honor the conventions that they make. If this law is not observed, then conventions lose their validity and the state of war is maintained. This law is the origin of justice. "Formally interpreted, it reinforces the claim that covenants oblige of themselves. Materially interpreted, it affirms that keeping covenants, as well as making them, is a condition of peace and so of preservation."[128]

The pact based on mutual trust is not valid because, for this purpose, a force is needed, one which would entail its observance. In the state of nature there is no justice, nor is there injustice, because justice means following a convention and injustice means breaking such a convention. The idea that the achievement of justice implies the existence of civil society can also be inferred from the definition of justice, such as it was understood by the classics, who believed that "justice is the constant will of giving to every man his own"[129], with a clear reference to Plato's *Republic*. As a result, where the is no "his/hers", there is no property, there is no injustice, and where there is no coercive power, meaning that there is no civil community, property is non-existent, since all individuals have equal claim to all the goods. Therefore, the nature of justice consists in the very action of establishing pacts, which however require a civil organization of society and

127 Ibid., chapter XIV, 31, p. 94 [71] [Hobbes's italics].

128 Gauthier, *Logic of Leviathan*, p. 56.

129 Hobbes, *Leviathan*, chapter XV, 3, p. 96 [72] [Hobbes's italics].

sufficient power to force men to abide by natural law. "For where no covenant hath preceded, there hath no right been transferred, and every man has right to every thing; and consequently, no action can be unjust. But when a covenant is made, then to break it is *unjust*: and the definition of *injustice*, is no other than *the not performance of covenant*."[130] Initially, there could be no other just attitude than the assiduous effort of keeping one's word, but what is just in this effort can never consist of the observance of the actual law, since there is no law in the real meaning of the word. The beginning of justice and property is contemporary with the organization of the state, because in order for these to exist, a coercive power is needed, one which forces men to honor their pacts. Contrary to the idea that natural laws do not lead to the preservation of the individual's life on Earth, but to the insurance of his eternal happiness, which means that promises that are contrary to this purpose may be broken, Hobbes believes that since we have no knowledge of the afterlife nor of the rewards that await the virtuous, breaking such a promise cannot be considered an act which follows the precepts of reason and those of nature. There are however, supporters of the idea that, although keeping a promise is a law of nature, certain exceptions may be allowed, like in the case of heretics or of those incapable of keeping a promise. Hobbes point out that admitting some exceptions goes against reason. The English philosopher distinguishes between the meanings of the words "just" and "unjust" depending on the subject that is attributed to them. Thus, if they are used in reference to men, they refer to "conformity, or inconformity of manners, to reason"[131]; if they are attributed to actions, they refer to the "conformity, or inconformity to reason, not of manners, or manner of life, but of particular actions". Depending on the justice of their actions, men are called innocent or guilty, they are not called just or unjust (injustice being seen as a sort of damage).

According to David Gauthier, the first three laws are sufficient for the understanding of the Hobbesian doctrine, since the "logic of Leviathan" could be resumed by the consideration of these laws: the other (there are sixteen) "make no substantial contribution to his moral doctrine."[132] Gauthier says that "we should, however, note the fourth," since this law is also a condition of peace. Just like justice is dependent on a prior convention, so *gratitude* (the fourth natural law) depends on a previous act of kindness. This law stipulates that someone who is granted an advantage by another must be grateful to the latter, meaning that they

130 Ibid., chapter XV, 2, p. 95 [71].
131 Ibid., chapter XV, 10, p. 98 [74].
132 Gauthier, *The Logic of Leviathan*, p. 56.

should never give them cause to regret the kindness they have shown. Breaking this law is called ingratitude and it means the perpetuation of the state of war. Some authors have pointed out that the law of gratitude is essential to understand the perpetration of the society, since this law is essential for understanding the parent-child relation in the Hobbesian doctrine of social contract. The key point is that human nature, which is deeply manifest with every child who is born, must be educated and prepared for the exercise of civil obligations. It is evident that a child is a human being; nevertheless, the child lacks the use of reason, so he is not part of an explicit convention and, therefore, has no obligation. The law of gratitude is therefore essential for explain and understand the *soft obligation* of children towards their parents. Through education the children learn the "logic of Leviathan", which is the logic of obeisance, against the arrogance; so the law of gratitude prepares the way of the justice.[133]

If we consider this point, we could not share the Gauthier's position, that "the further laws of nature play no significant role in Hobbes's moral theory, and none at all in his political theory."[134] In our view, the other laws of nature are of greatest importance for understand, firstly, that the sociability, which is no natural, is a social construction rooted in the laws of right reason and, secondly, that the Leviathan is "the king of all the children of pride."[135] For this reason, we present all the sixteen laws of nature.

The fifth natural law is that of *complaisance*, which makes men strive *to live in harmony with others.*[136] Those who respect this law can be called sociable, while the rest are "stubborn, insociable, froward [perverse], intractable."[137] *Forgiveness* is the sixth natural law and it asks that we forgive the offences brought to us by those who now repent; from a sign of peace it is turned into a sign of fear – but even so, it must be granted, because otherwise it represents a sign of aversion towards peace (towards the first law of nature). The seventh law dictates that, in

---

133 As Howard Warrender noticed, "one of the most important considerations regarding Hobbes's law of gratitude is its relevance for his theory of 'tacit covenant'. Hobbes's doctrine is mainly concerned, not with the keeping of promises as such, but with the keeping of covenants, and his law of justice is framed accordingly." Howard Warrender, *The Political Philosophy of Hobbes: His Theory of Obligation* (Oxford: Oxford University Press, 1957), pp. 51.

134 Gauthier, *Logic of Leviathan*, p. 56.

135 Hobbes, *Leviathan*, chapter XXVIII, 27, p. 212 [167].

136 This law is present in *De Cive* as *let every man render himself useful unto others* (see Hobbes, *De Cive*, chapter III, § 9, p. 66).

137 Hobbes, *Leviathan*, chapter XV, 17, p. 101 [76].

the act of revenge (understood as *answering he who has harmed us with harm*), one must take into account the future good, not the past evil. Therefore, punishment is only admitted to provided that, by its means, we better the one who has wronged us or we make an example out of him for others. To cause someone suffering with no reason is called cruelty and by it, man tends to reinstate the state of nature. The eighth natural law is expounded *against insolence*, namely: no one may express hatred or contempt towards others. Next comes six laws considered by the specialists in Hobbesian political philosophy as the most important ones concerning equality,[138] the ones which he calls laws of natural equality, since they refer directly to the issue of equality.

The first of these – and the ninth in Hobbes's order – is *against arrogance*. The English philosopher starts from the idea that all men are equal by nature, which means that in the circumstances which precede the institution of civil society a matter like "who is the best" has no relevance. When enouncing this law, he makes mention of the Aristotelian political theory, which supported slavery, therefore inequality, as a natural fact. This would mean that the master – slave relation is not set by conventions, it is given by the difference between wisdom, a fact which Hobbes believes to go *not only against reason, but also against experience*, "for there are very few so foolish, that had not rather govern themselves, than be governed by others."[139] People can only enter the state of peace, meaning to establish civil society, if they are all equals, therefore every man must think of every other man as his equal by nature.

"The man who demands more for himself than he allows to others is arrogant. since he refuses to accept obligations which he insists others must accept as a condition of peace."[140] The tenth law refers to the main consequence of arrogance, which makes some men to take on more roles, to the detriment of others. Hobbes calls this *arrogance*. Once the state of peace is established, no one can claim any right which others cannot have. When civil society is constituted, men must give up part of their natural rights, more to the point, the freedom of doing whatever they want, but at the same time it is necessary to keep certain rights, in order to preserve their life. For example, they will keep the right over their own bodies and over all things necessary for survival. However, if upon entering the state of peace some get to keep more rights than others, then not only this law is

138 See B. Baumrin, "Hobbes's egalitarianism: The laws of natural equality", in *Thomas Hobbes, de la méthaphysique à la politique: Collque franco-americain de Nantes*, sous al direction de Martin Bertman et Michel Malherbe (Paris: Vrin, 1989), p. 121.

139 Hobbes, *Leviathan*, chapter XV, 21, p. 102 [77].

140 Gauthier, *The Logic of Leviathan*, p. 57.

broken, but also the previous one. These who break the law are called arrogant people, while those who follow it are modest.[141] One thing worth noting about this law of nature is that it becomes applicable as soon as we enter the state of peace, which means that it does not exist in the state of nature, but merely at the beginning of civil society and it determines the terms of the agreement (of the contract). The source of this law is constituted by equality among men. Vain and arrogant people break the very terms of a possible peace, thinking of themselves as exceptions and thus breaking with natural equality.

The eleventh natural law concerning equity demands that "if a man be trusted to judge between man and man"[142], he must judge them equally. Otherwise, misunderstandings between men cannot be trialed through war. To judge equally means, first of all, to be impartial, and not necessarily to make an equal distribution in any controversy. From the law of equity ensues the next law, the one that refers to the common employment of all things that cannot be distributed. When quantity allows this, employment must be unlimited, and when it does not, it must be proportional to the number of people who have the right to use it, otherwise distribution would be unequal and equity would not be preserved. There are, however, certain things which cannot be divided, nor used in common. In this case, equity (which we have seen Hobbes interpret as equal distribution), demands that the entire possession be decided by ballot; "other means of equal distribution cannot be imagined."[143]

The fourteenth law suggests three formal processes of distribution, starting from the distinction between *arbitrary* and *natural* odds. The odds are arbitrary and the rules are set according to the agreement of the participants. Natural odds can in turn be of two types, namely primogeniture of first occupancy, the latter being particularly important. Through his theory concerning the first occupant, Hobbes can be thought of as the precursor of Locke's theory on property. The matter which is raised concerning the rule of first occupancy is that it might give birth to a process of violent competition, one which resembles the one found in the state of nature. Locke will try to resolve this difficulty by appealing to an additional clause, which stipulates that the first occupant becomes the legitimate owner only if by occupying that land he leaves land which is "still enough, and as good left" for the others[144].

---

141 Hobbes, *Leviathan*, chapter XV, 22, p. 102 [77].

142 Ibid., chapter XV, 23, p. 102 [77].

143 Ibid., chapter XV, 26, p. 103 [78].

144 Locke, *Two Treatises of Government*, p. 291. [Second Treatise, § 33].

The fifteenth natural law is the one concerning *the safety of the means for peace*. No matter how willing people are to follow natural laws, there may arise, however, questions concerning one action or another (first, it has been accomplished and then if it was done according to the law; the first question is *de facto*, and the second, *de jure*). Therefore, another natural law must be enunciated, the one concerning the right to seek *arbitration* when misunderstandings may occur between the two parties, concerning certain rights. This one ensues the next two natural laws, one which says that no one can be *his own judge*, and the second, which states that no one can be a judge if there is a cause which would make him *biased* (for example a reward, be it material, symbolic or esthetic). The last natural law refers to *the use of witnesses* when dealing with controversies of fact. These are the natural laws that assert peace as a means of preserving the lives of men in society and that only take into account civil society. Although Hobbes points out that there are other things, like lack of measure, which can lead to the destruction of separate individuals and which should also be among the things forbidden by natural law, he believes them to be of lesser importance from the perspective of the construction of civil society. All the laws of nature can be understood if we consider the Christian saying: "Do not that to another, which thou wouldest not have done to thyself."[145] Hobbes believes this to be a kind of "rule, by which the laws of nature may easily be examined." Through it, the actions of others can be compared to our own. It does not imply that we should put ourselves in other people's shoes (which is actually quite hard to do), but to consider the actions of others as we would our own and to imagine our own actions as if others had done them[146]. The essential part refers to our own person (not on the other party), in its two instances: examining our own actions from our own point of view and examining the other party's actions as if they were our own. The question is not: "would I have done this if I was that person?", but: "would I let that person do this to me in the given situation?" Thus, we can understand how the above stated rule allows us to evaluate the laws of nature as particular rules, applicable in different situations and to establish which of them are rational and which are not. The rational rules are the ones according to which men (agents) are treated as equals; the irrational ones are the biased ones.

145 Hobbes, *Leviathan*, chapter XV, 35, p. 104 [79].

146 That means that I can complain about the unjust action that I have suffered at the hands of the other person; in the same way he is entitled to complain about the unjust action that he has suffered at my hands.

The laws of nature always bind the man in his conscience, but they only bind him in real life when there is security, meaning in a state run society.[147] They are not principles which show us how we should behave; they are scientific laws, meaning statements about how human nature should be conducted. Natural laws are eternal and immutable, since injustice, ingratitude, arrogance, pride, inequity, bias cannot be considered legitimate and, furthermore, it is impossible for war to preserve life and for peace to destroy it. These laws are easy to follow and all they require is desire and exertion: "constant and lasting"[148] in order to be fulfilled. The science of laws is the only moral philosophy, since it is none other than the science of good and evil in human society.

Hobbes distinguishes "no less precisely than any other moralist between legality and morality"[149]. It is not the lawfulness, but the morality of an action which makes man just. A just man is one who complies with the law because it is the law, because he feels obligated by it *in foro interno* and not by the fear of punishment or in order to gain reputation[150].

By claiming that a moral attitude, conscience, intent are more important than action, Hobbes's point of view is in accordance with that of Christian tradition, this being a fact which Hobbes himself asserts in *De Cive*: "Lawes of Nature had regard chiefly unto Conscience."[151]

In the state of nature, the distinction between just and unjust acts depends exclusively on the judgment of individual consciousness. Essentially, any action which the individual's conscience recognizes as necessary for self-preservation is allowed and any action which is undertaken without this purpose is forbidden. Or, following this paradigm, we can say that in the state of nature, all actions can be deemed necessary for self-preservation. However, if in the state of nature any action is allowed, this does not mean that any intention is permitted: the only allowed intention is the one directed towards self-preservation.[152] Therefore, it can

---

147 As it is pointed out by much modern interpreters, the natural have to deal with individual's pursuit of self-preservation, but "without a doubt talk of natural law carried a presumption that securing the common good was the proper function of the Law of Nature." S.A. Lloyd, *Morality in the Philosophy of Thomas Hobbes: Cases in the Law of Nature* (Cambridge: Cambridge University Press, 2009), p. 111.

148 Hobbes, *Leviathan*, chapter XV, 12, p. 114 [87].

149 Strauss, *Political Philosophy of Hobbes*, p. 23.

150 See Hobbes, *Elements of Law*, I, chapter XVI, § 4, p. 89. See also Hobbes, *De Cive*, chapter III, § 5, p. 64, and chapter IV, § 21, p. 83.

151 Hobbes, *De Cive*, chapter IV, § 21, p. 83.

152 Strauss, *Political Philosophy of Hobbes*, p. 24.

be said that the distinction between just and unjust intentions is valid even in the state of nature and therefore, it has absolute validity[153].

The origin of a just intention is the fear of a violent death. Just is merely what man does out of fear of death, since he is aware of his weakness, honestly revealing to himself and to others his weakness and his fear of dying, without any thought for his ego, since the latter can only be the origin of an unjust attitude[154]. "Briefly, in the state of nature, what's just, and unjust, is not to be esteem'd by the Actions, but by the Counsell, and Conscience of the Actor. That which is done out of necessity, out of endeavour for peace, for the preservation of our selves, is done with Right."[155]

Hobbes's purpose is to show that conscience and fear of a violent death is one and the same thing. This allows him to systematically and legitimately distinguish between right and wrong, between moral and immoral motives, between the attitude of the unjust man who obeys the (civil) laws out of fear of punishment, lacking all internal conviction, and the attitude of the just man, who obeys the laws out of the fear of dying, and therefore due to an internal conviction. Only the realization of the threat of imminent death can determine man to free himself from his natural vanity. For that matter, "the foundation of Hobbes's political philosophy is constituted by the moral opposition between fundamentally unjust vanity and the fundamentally just fear of a violent death"[156]. At the end of chapter XV in the *Leviathan*, Hobbes explicitly denies the existence of a natural law which unconditionally binds men in the state of nature. "These dictates of reason, men used to call by the name of laws; but improperly: for they are but conclusions, or theorems concerning what conduceth to the conservation and defence of themselves; whereas law, properly is the word of him, that by right hath command over others"[157]. The law implies obligation, but obligation only arises based on conventions between men which were previously free and had no ties between them, which means that it is limited to civil society.[158] Getting

153 Although in chapter XIII of the *Leviathan* Hobbes states that "To this war of every man against every man, this also is In such a war consequent; that nothing can be unjust," Hobbes, *Leviathan*, chapter 13, § 13, p. 83 [63], Leo Strauss believes that through this statement Hobbes was referring to actions, not to intentions. See Strauss, *The Political Philosophy of Hobbes*, p. 24.

154 See Hobbes, *Elements of Law*, I, chapter 9, § 1, p. 50.

155 Hobbes, *De Cive*, chapter III, § 27, annotation, p. 73.

156 Strauss, *Political Philosophy of Hobbes*, p. 52.

157 Hobbes, *Leviathan*, chapter XV, 41, p. 106 [80].

158 As Ross Harrison points out, the problem with the concept of law of nature in Hobbes is "if the law of nature [is] really a law in itself, or does it only become a law

from the state of war to the state of peace can only be done by acknowledging the natural equality which thus becomes a natural law ensued from reason.

2.3 The institution of civil society

In order to overcome the state of nature there has to be a power which compels men to obey the same rules; there is no other way for the common good. Natural laws are of no help if they are not supported by an authority which determines people to observe these laws, since "covenants, without the sword, are but words, and of no strength to secure a man at all."[159] Therefore, in the absence of a common power, each man will rely on his own strength in order to defend himself from others. Even if people were to come together in a group against a common enemy, in the absence of a common power they will still act according to their own interests. As a result, they could not expect protection neither against a common enemy, nor from the harm they could inflict on one another. This happens because of the differences in opinion concerning how they should act. Consequently, their strength diminishes and they can be easily defeated by an enemy, or, if there are no enemies, they might end up fighting among themselves in order to achieve their own interests. If, in the absence of a common power, people would consent to obey natural laws, this would mean that peace can be maintained in the absence of submission and, as a result, civil community would no longer be needed. Since some creatures, like bees or ants, live together in harmony, although they are governed by instinct and they do not poses an articulate language; we may ask if this could not be the case for mankind as well. Hobbes's answer follows a series of arguments: 1) men are always competing for fame and distinctions, which leads them to envy and hatred, and finally to war; 2) men make a distinction between common and individual goods, and, since they enjoy comparing themselves to one another, they make efforts to obtain private goods; 3) men do not lack reason and therefore, each thinks that he is more intelligent and more capable of governing political matters, which leads to disunity and to civil war; 4) the existence of articulate language means that good and evil can be dissimulated any time; 5) mindless creatures cannot distinguish between being

---

when there is a state to enforce it". According to Harrison, "Hobbes's laws seem to have a hypothetical form. They are what people should do if, and only if, they can be sure that others will do it as well." Ross Harrison, *Hobbes, Locke, and Confusion's Masterpiece: An Examination of Seventeenth-Century Political Philosophy* (Cambridge: Cambridge University Press, 2003), pp. 71–72.

159 Hobbes, *Leviathan*, chapter XVII, 2, p. 111 [85].

harmed and suffering a loss, so they have no quarrel with their peers. As far as human are concerned, the less worries they have, the more tempted they are to start trouble, for in this situation they wish to exhibit their wisdom; 6) understanding among animals is a natural one, while among men, it is an artificial one, which means that apart from the initial convention, there has to be a greater power which makes the agreement steadfast and durable.

The only way to attain such common power, capable of defending people from the attacks of foreigners and from the harm they can inflict each other, providing them the indispensable security for a satisfactory way of life, is to transfer their entire power and strength to one man or to an assembly of men. In other words, they need to name a man or an assembly of men in order to represent them; each man should recognize his own will in the actions of that person or assembly, in those actions which concern common peace and security. As far as these things are concerned there can be only one will and only one judgment, that belonging to the holder of the power. This act by which the nomination of a single person is accomplished equates the signing of a genuine contract, of which these are the essential words: "I authorize and give up my right of governing myself, to this man, or to this assembly of men, on this condition, that thou give up thy right to him, and authorize all his actions in like manner."[160]

Once this convention is concluded, the group of people, thus reunited in one person, is called a civil community or *Civitas*. This corresponds to the birth of the great Leviathan[161] or of the mortal God, to which we owe, under the rule of the immortal God, our peace and our protection. Therefore, the great state or the great Leviathan can be seen as a single person, and its interests are different from those of the individuals. The state must not be mistaken for a single citizen, nor for group of citizens together; it is a person the will of which must be considered, according to the concluded agreement, as the will of all individuals and which can make use of the strength and of the means of all individuals for the sake of peace and of common defense. By comparing the biblical Leviathan and the state, Hobbes refers to the fact that the state is the great power which subdues those who break with natural equality (and, thus, make the state of peace

160 Ibid., chapter XVII, 13, p. 113 [87].

161 According to the Old Testament, the Leviathan designates a fantastic marine monster. On the cover of the 1651 edition of the *Leviathan* a giant is depicted, whose body is made up of many men, holding a sword in his right hand and a crutch in his left hand, ruling over the entire country and over all of its institutions: civil, military, ecclesiastic. Above him there is the inscription: "There is no power on Earth such as this" (*The Book of Job*, 41. 24).

impossible).[162] Only the state can subdue vanity in the end, since its *raison d'être* is the suppression of man's natural appetite, meaning his pride, his ambition and his vanity. According to this interpretation, Hobbes's *Leviathan* is "the measure of justice and the end of ambition."[163]

Hobbes does not explain the transition from the state of nature to the civil state of a community; he merely asserts its existence. The proof that such a transition is possible is provided by the simple fact that organized communities or states really exist. Hobbes only tells that the state can be formed by acquisition or by institution. Thus, we have the distinction between the natural and the artificial state, between the "republics by acquisition" – based on the natural force of the father or of the conqueror – and the "republic by institution" – the result of a volunteer submission to a chosen form of government, an artificially established one. "The attaining to this sovereign power, is by two ways. One, by natural force; as when a man maketh his children, to submit themselves, and their children to his government, as being able to destroy them if they refuse; or by war subdueth his enemies to his will, giving them their lives on that condition. The other, is when men agree amongst themselves, to submit to some man, or assembly of men, voluntarily, on confidence to be protected by him against all others."[164] In the first case, we are dealing with a natural form of domination, since people "submit themselves to another for feare,"[165] the resulting political body being then "paternal and despotic."[166] In the second case, the origin of society lies in a conscious intention, the resulting political body "is called a commonwealth"[167] and is "institutive, which may be also called politicall."[168] In this case, a number

162 It is to be noticed that, in the *Bible* (Old Testament, The Book of Job), the "Leviathan" was designated as the king of the arrogant men. Explaining the meaning of the Hobbesian political metaphor, Carl Schmitt have explained why Hobbes make use of the image of the biblical monster: "In the political situation of the seventeenth century, that is, in the struggle between absolute state power and the authority of the nobility and the church, the leviathan according to this explanation no longer projects an image of the highest, indivisible, and strongest temporal power, one in accord with the biblical symbol of the most powerful animal." Carl Schmitt, The *Leviathan in the State Theory of Thomas Hobbes: Meaning and Failure of a Political Symbol* (Westport and London: Greenwood Press, 1996), p. 20.

163 Strauss, *Political Philosophy of Hobbes*, p. 33.

164 Hobbes, *Leviathan*, chapter XVII, 15, pp. 114–115 [88].

165 Hobbes, *De Cive*, chapter V, § 12, p. 90.

166 Hobbes, *Elements of Law*, I, chapter XIX, § 11, p. 108.

167 Ibid.

168 Hobbes, *De Cive*, chapter V, § 12, p. 90.

of men agree to transfer their rights to a third party, namely the sovereign, and enter into a contractual form of cooperation; thus they institute the sovereignty and become subjects or citizens. This means that each subject is supposed to be in observance of the rules of the sovereign and not to resist his power, but only to the extent that all individuals transfer their rights in the same way, also promising not to oppose the political power. Therefore, this power is the equivalent of an absolute right over all things. In other words, civil power is identical to absolute power. According to Hobbes, sovereignty by institution is not completely different than sovereignty by acquisition: in the first case "men who choose their sovereign, do it for fear of one another,"[169] while in the last case they "subject themselves, to him they are afraid of."[170] So the artificial state can emerge there where two adversaries who both fear for their lives overcome their vanity and shame, in confessing their fear, and acknowledge that their true enemy is not their rival, but "that terrible enemy of nature, death"[171], the common foe who forces them into mutual understanding and union. But the way in which sovereignty emerges is less important as long as it is acknowledged by all citizens. Both the sovereign by victory and the sovereign by institution have the same rights and their subjects have the same obligations. According to Hobbes, the foundation of the state is neither divine law, nor patriarchal law, not even the law of force; he thinks that the principle of legitimation of political order is the consent of the subjects. However, we should not consider him as a partisan of the sovereignty of the people, in the sense of constitutional philosophy of right. The crowd is the source of sovereignty as long as it stands as a multitude of subjects; it is nothing in itself, politically speaking. If each individual preserves what is his own, the crowd no longer possesses anything. When it is said that the people have taken up arms, the statement is inexact, since the city cannot be in revolt against itself. As long as there is no institution of civil order, the crowd remains in the state of nature, and there can be no question of justice, nor question of property, because there is no security. Sovereignty does not reside in the crowd,

---

169 Hobbes, *Leviathan*, chapter XX, 2, p. 132 [102].

170 Ibid. As we have pointed out in a previous paper, "the cornerstone of the [Hobbesian] theory of sovereignty is the profound relation between the domination through institution and the domination through acquisition" since in Hobbes "there is a double movement between institution and acquisition, not in the exercise of effective sovereignty, but in the discourse about sovereignty". Corneliu Bilba and Gabriela Ratulea, "Suveranitate şi violenţă la Hobbes şi Foucault", in *Violenţa. Aspecte psihosociale*, edit. Gilles Ferréol and Adrian Neculau (Iaşi: Polirom, 2003), p. 33.

171 Hobbes, *Elements of Law I*, XIV, § 6, p. 79.

but in the state, and it comes into existence only when the state is embodied by one person. By denying the sovereignty of the multitude (which is in contradiction of the principles of democratic conceptions), Hobbes expressly states that the primitive act which generates the civil society is *not a contract between the crowd and the sovereign*; the contract is only concluded between the members of a multitude who pledge to one another not to oppose the person or the persons invested with sovereign authority. This mutual contract cannot bind the sovereign in any way. By promising not to oppose sovereign power, people accept the will of the sovereign as their own; they will want whatever He wants. Therefore the institution of civil power is alienation, not a delegation.

In order to speak of a pact between two persons, they must become parties, and this is not the case here, in the relation between the sovereign and his subjects. Before the institution of the state there is only one party, which is the crowd, and after the institution, the crowd is dissolved through the very act of institution. Thus, at any given time, only one of the two parties exists and consequently, a pact between the two parties is impossible. Therefore, the pact which institutes the sovereignty is not concluded between the sovereign and his subjects, but merely between the subjects and it stipulates that they will accept whatever the ruling power decides. The pact can be explicit (in writing) or implicit (as in the case of conquered countries), but there is no consensus in the sense that John Locke latter will assign it, when he will speak of a contract between the sovereign and his subjects. Concluding, the pact is the subjects' only political act. Their role is to obey, and the sovereign's is to protect them. Legally and politically speaking, there is no limit for sovereignty in Hobbes's system. There is no right to rebellion, since the sovereign is not limited by contract and didn't even participate in the elaboration of the contract. The subjects only hold those legal rights which the sovereign guarantees. He is the only legislator, he is not subject to civil law and his will is the one that grants authority to the law. He holds the power to censor any expression of opinion, to assign private property, to determine what is just and what is unjust, good or bad, legal or illegal. He also holds the right to judge, to choose peace or war, to choose the officers of the nation, to mete out punishments and offer rewards, to decide in moral and political matters, as well as to decide how God shall be worshiped. Among these rights, three of them are essential for understanding Hobbesian absolutism: 1) the right to establish by legal means what is just and what is unjust; 2) the right to censor any expression of opinion; 3) the right to assign private property.

With regard to the first point, we should say that the right in question highlights the difference between the state of nature and the state of civil society. In the first case, the individual decides for himself what must be done and what must be avoided and, as a result, everything is permitted for him and nothing is just or unjust. Since in civil society the individual renounces his right over all things, he also abandons the choice of what must be avoided and what must be sought. Consequently, the state which has inherited all the rights of the individuals is now the only body capable of deciding what is allowed and what is forbidden. Since, by the covenant they made, the individuals have bound themselves to obey the state and justice is nothing more than the observance of conventions, submitting oneself to the authority of the state is just and not doing so is unjust. Therefore, the political authority has the obligation to determine what theft, adultery and crime are. For example, in the states where polygamy is permitted, we cannot speak of adultery, just like we cannot call murder the act of a soldier who kills an enemy in war.

Concerning the right to censor any expression of opinion, we have to mention that, since the state power has to provide peace, it must repress any opinion, any doctrine which promotes resistance to its laws. Thus, the sovereign has the right to pass judgment concerning all opinions and to allow their publication or not. As for the right to assign property, it is obvious that property did not exist before the constitution of the state and comes into existence only with the rule of law. In the state of nature, each held an absolute right over all things without having any exclusive right over anything. But, by transferring all rights when constituting civil community, the state naturally became the only owner, and each individual's right over his possession is nothing more than a concession granted by the state.

Since power has such rights, it is clear that no many rights are acknowledged for the subjects. According to the initial contract they are employees and they cannot denounce this contract in order to conclude a new one, unless the sovereign agrees to do so. For the same reason, subjects cannot dismiss their sovereign under the claim of poor administration, since the sovereign is the representative of the city. If we assume that he has violated the pact, no one is entitled to judge this dispute. Since no one can pass judgment, this means there is anarchy and return to the state of nature; if the state has to do the judging, that means that the task falls to the sovereign, as he is the representative of the state. It is true that he has become sovereign through the general will, but this does not mean that the crowd can depose him, because there is no legitimacy: once civil society was instated, the civil power comes into existence as the only legitimate one. The subjects no longer have any power to use against their sovereign, since their powers were transferred to him.[172]

172 This is what Foucault have called a "mechanism of power", meaning that "power is indeed the implementation and deployment of a relationship of force" and "power is

According to the classical tradition of political philosophy, sovereignty can take on three forms, namely: monarchy, aristocracy and democracy. The other apparent forms merely reflect attitudes towards the initial three (for example, if one dislikes monarchy, one will call it tyranny). Concerning the forms of sovereignty, Hobbes points out that, in the transition from the democratic state to the monarchic state, there is no contract between the state and the monarch, just as there was no contract between the crowds and the sovereign in the transition from the state of nature to the civil state. Among the different forms of government, the English philosopher prefers absolute monarchy, because he believes that it constitutes the best means of maintaining peace. As to absolutism, Hobbes was probably influenced by Robert Fimer's conception,[173] who believed monarchy to be an institution of divine law, one to which the people should submit unconditionally. According to Hobbes, monarchy is the only form of government in which the interests of the monarch and of his subjects coincide. What is good for the monarch is good for his people. Monarchy is to be preferred to aristocracy and to democracy, since the monarch has fewer favorites than an assembly, and also, it is easier for him to receive advice from an assembly. This means that decisions are easier to make. There are no divide fractions and the threat of war is greatly diminished. It is true that, under monarchy, there can be matters of succession, but these can be avoided if the will of the sovereign is respected. Hobbes shows his strongest support of ab solute monarchy in *De Cive*, where he

essentially that which represses." Michel Foucault, *Society must be defended: Lecture at the College de France, 1975–76* (New York: Picador, 2003), p. 15.

173 The work of Filmer, *Patriarcha*, which was written between 1620 and 1642, was published only posthumously, in 1680 (Hobbes died in 1679 and *The Leviathan* was published in 1651). It seems that Filmer's treaty circulated in manuscripts and Hobbes know it (or he known the published works of Filmer, like *The necessity of the absolute power of all kings*, from 1648) since in *Leviathan* he modified his conception on patrimonial kingdom which have been developed in *Elements of Law* (written in 1640). Namely, in *Elements*, the patrimonial sovereignty was not been considered as founded on the consent, while in *Leviathan* Hobbes says that every submission to a master who provide security and peace is a covenant. The purpose of Hobbes in this controversy is to demonstrate, against the patriarchalists, than a woman could be king and that, "in the state of nature, dominion over children is naturally the mother's." Sharon A. Lloyd and Susanne Sreedhar, "Hobbes's Moral and Political Philosophy," *The Stanford Encyclopedia of Philosophy*, 2014, paragraph 11. For an analysis of Hobbesian ideas in historical context, see Jon Parkin, *Taming the Leviathan: The Reception of the Political and Religious Ideas of Thomas Hobbes in England 1640–1700* (Cambridge: Cambridge University Press, 2007), p. 107 and sq.

tries to argue, with the means of tradition, about the best form of government: "the whole universe is governed by one God; that the Ancients preferr'd the Monarchicall state before all others, ascribing the Rule of the Gods to one Jupiter; that in the beginning of affairs, and of Nations, the decrees of Princes were held for Laws; that paternall government instituted by God himselfe in the Creation, was Monarchicall; that other governments were compacted by the artifice of men out of the ashes of Monarchy, after it had been ruined with seditions; and that the people of God were under the jurisdiction of Kings"[174]. Even in democracies or aristocracies, in times of war, the entire power is entrusted to the leader of the army[175], which leads us to the conclusion that a difficult situation can only be successfully managed by a single person, the power of the general-in-command being proof of the excellence of royal domination.

Unlike *De Cive, The Elements* and *The Leviathan* treat of the possibility of a limited monarchy. This is the case of the elective monarchy, in which kings can be elected, which means that they can only use power (not own it) for a certain period of time. Moreover, in this case, people do not transfer all of their rights to the sovereign, but keep certain rights, like the right to gather together and to question the king's decisions[176]. Without a doubt, this type of monarchy is not an authentic one; it is more like a mandate given to the king by the sovereign people. Such a monarchy is explicitly excluded in *De Cive,* where it is stated that sovereignty rights belong exclusively to the monarch and any promise or pact which could obstruct him to exercise his sovereign power is void[177].

In all these works, Hobbes first takes into account the artificial state, and only then he considers the natural dominion, paternal or despotic. While discussing the sovereignty, he examines the particular case of the monarchy by institution, thus artificial. A single difference occurs in Hobbes's analysis: while in *The Leviathan* the right of succession is seen as a specific problem of monarchy when discussing the republic by institution, in his prior works that right is mentioned in the context of discussions about the state of nature. This is so because, from Hobbes's point of view, the natural monarchy and the state of nature were one and the same thing[178].

174 Hobbes, *De Cive*, chapter X, § 3, p. 131.

175 Ibid., chapter X, § 7, p. 180.

176 Hobbes, *Elements of Law*, II, chapter XXI, § 10, p. 123.

177 It must be mentioned that in the preface to *De Cive* (1642), which was compiled later on (1646), Hobbes has proven to be more moderate, stating that the superiority of monarchy is only likely, it hasn't been proven.

178 Thus, while in the *Leviathan* this subject is exposed in chapter XIX entitled *Of several Kinds of Commonwealth by Institution; and of Succession to the Sovereign Power*,

With regard to the natural dominion, this can be of two types: *despotic*, which is constituted through conquest, and *paternal,* which is based on the authority of the fathers in their natural families. As to the monarchy which Hobbes initially identifies with the state of nature, it is understood that it is a paternal and not a despotic form of domination, Hobbes's claiming being that paternal dominion (thus patriarchal monarchy) is the foundation – if not in the legal sense, then at least in the historical sense – of all the states, or of most of them[179]. Even in *The Leviathan*, it is obvious that the rule of succession in the monarchy is derived from the rights of the fathers in the natural families, since the sovereign of the civil state is still in the state of nature and – as Hobbes says – a family is like a little kingdom, as a kingdom is like a great family. However, Hobbes separates the patriarchal monarchy from the artificial one. Although in respect to the relation between the monarch and his subjects he notes, in passing, that they "are to him as his children and servants"[180], it does not mean that the two types of monarchy can be mistaken for one another: "for the King, though as a father of children, and a master of domestic servants, yet he commands the people in general never but by a precedent law, and as a politic, not a natural person."[181]

If we should distinguish between the natural state and the artificial one, it is because the former is a monarchy, while the latter can as well be democratic or aristocratic. In *De Corpore Politico*, Hobbes claims that democracy had been the initial form of the artificial state. The anteriority of democracy compared to all other forms of government is thought of as a necessity. This is so because aristocracy and monarchy imply the existence of a contract between the sovereign and his subjects, which is impossible in the case of democracy, "for it cannot be imagined, that the multitude should contract with itself, or with any one man, or number of men, parcel of itself, to make itself sovereign."[182] In *De Cive*, this thesis has lost much of its meaning, while in *The Leviathan*, it is missing. A remainder of this conception is also present in *Behemoth* where Hobbes, in reference to the first political communities in England, says that "a man…, should be made

---

in *De Cive* it is exposed in chapter IX, *Of the rights which Parents have over their children, and of a Kingdome Paternall*, and in *Elements of Law,* part II, *De corpore politico*, chapter IV *Of the Power of Fathers, and of Patrimonial Kingdom.*

179 See Hobbes, *Leviathan*, chapter XX, pp. 130–132 and chapter XXII, pp. 153–154; see also Hobbes, *Behemoth*, p. 347.

180 Hobbes, *Elements of Law*, II, chapter XXIII, § 12, p. 134; see also Hobbes, *De Cive*, chapter IX, § 14, p. 127.

181 Hobbes, *Behemoth*, I, p. 227.

182 Hobbes, *Elements of Law*, II, chapter XXI, § 2, p. 118.

acquainted, and be of council, with him that hath the sovereignty in matter of government, and have the greatest and most honourable offices both in peace and war."[183] No matter if it is an initial form of political organization or not, democracy remains for Hobbes the worst form of government, with minimum odds of insuring peace and security. He believes monarchy to be the only capable of accomplishing this goal, which was ultimately the purpose for which the Leviathan had been instituted.

2.3.1 The constitution of civil power

In the historical interpretation of the state of nature, the individuals who submit themselves to the authority of the Leviathan are rational beings, who have known the insecurity and the misery of the state of nature and who freely desire to shelter themselves from any threat of war. If they freely submit to a political authority they do not do so in order to be subjects to a new form of insecurity, but precisely in order to escape from it. Advocate of absolutism, Hobbes states the existence of certain limitations to the powers of the state, even more frequently than the general image of his doctrine might suggest[184]. Thus, if the individual's physical integrity or his freedom of movement is threatened, he retains the invaluable right to defend himself even against the public force, and this right is in accordance with the first natural law.

The degree of submission depends on the way in which the sovereign exercises the power which he has been entrusted with. Although he possesses absolute power, he must use it rationally. Otherwise, the individuals might estimate that they have gone back to the state of nature and that any act is permitted for the preservation of their life and security.

The sovereign is granted absolute power concerning the means in which he can use it in order to preserve the peace and security of his subjects[185]. For Hobbes, the rebellion constitutes the supreme evil. In the *Leviathan*, he suggests a different pattern for the relation between command and obedience, one centered on the existing bond between the calculation of individual interests, the process

183 Hobbes, *Behemoth*, II, pp. 259–260.
184 Pierre Manent, *Naissance de la politique moderne: Machiavel/Hobbes/Rousseau* (Paris: Editions Payot, 1977), Deuxième partie: «Hobbes», Chapitre II [consulted in Romanian translation, p. 111].
185 For example, he has the freedom to institute a new tax, in order to fortify the frontiers, without anybody being able to question that right.

by which authority is formed and political representation.[186] The argument which serves as a starting point is that the positive satisfaction of interests requires each citizen to acknowledge the political authority. The political representation of interests becomes the instrument which allows the neutralization of the selfish nature of each private interest. Thus, the state becomes the place where protection and submission are exchanged, this being an exchange which constitutes the very grounding of sovereign authority. In order to be represented, any private interest has to be reported to sovereignty and to acknowledge absolute power. This, however, does not mean that the sovereign can act arbitrarily, he is responsible for his actions, but in a different manner than it is understood by responsible action in our present day. In modern democracies, the holders of power must answer to public opinion, meaning to the people, to the only true holder of sovereignty. The people can sanction power in different manners, the elections being the most important of these manners. If the voters estimate that the representatives of power have failed to do their duty, by vote they can transfer the power to other individuals who they believe to be more capable or more honest. In Hobbes, the idea of such a responsibility of political power towards the people is missing. For him, the people does not exist without the sovereign, so there is no sovereign people to which the monarch must give an account for the way in which he has dealt with public affairs. At most, we can say that the monarch is responsible to himself, which does not mean that much, politically speaking. Hobbes's political argument against the monarch's responsibility towards the people starts from the assumption of dividing sovereignty between the monarch and the parliament and, also, of making the first responsible before the latter. In this case, we can expect ambitious parliamentarians to constantly attack royal power, aiming to take on certain prerogatives of the latter, which would obviously be unacceptable for the monarch, making the risk of civil war imminent. This is why the question of the Parliament's responsibility arises. If the people is not sovereign, as Hobbesian doctrine assumes, then there is no responsibility of the Parliament before any political body. Therefore, a choice must be made between the monarch and the Parliament. Obviously, Hobbes prefers the first option,[187] since the monarch is not supposed to be divided against himself as the Parliament could be.

Although he does not answer to people, the monarch "answers to God"[188] in respect to his mission to ensure the security of the people. He is bound by the

186 See Luc Foisneau, *Politique, Droit et Théologie chez Bodin, Grotius et Hobbes* (Paris : Kimé, 1997), p. 21.

187 Hobbes, *Leviathan*, chapter XXIX, p. 216, and chapter XXII, p. 153.

188 Ibid., chapter XLII, p. 357.

natural law and must answer to the creator of that law, meaning to God. If the sovereign is not subject to positive laws, since he is the source of these laws, and he promulgates or annuls them according to political and social demands, he is still bound to follow the natural laws created by God, to whom he is a subject, by his mortal nature. If the transfer of rights which have constitute sovereignty has placed him above the other mortals, yet it has not changed his mortal nature, so he owes submission to God.

In order to leave the state of nature, the individuals were rationally determined to renounce their right of waging war; nevertheless, the sovereign has by definition the right to wage war against them in case of rebellion, or against any enemy of the state. No individual has the right to punish the sovereign, who in turn has the right to punish any individual. The social contract is therefore a covenant concerning the institution of "monopoly of legitimate violence,"[189] since peace and security in the state can only be ensured with the price of this asymmetry. If the sovereign didn't have the right to use violence against those who violate the covenant, there would be a return to the state of nature. Even if the sovereign keeps his right of starting war, he is still bound by the obligation to use this right responsibly, being limited by the laws of nature. Therefore, we can state that the sovereign should try to live in peace with his subjects, knowing that he only answers to God for his actions. This assignation is not without importance, since it excludes the possibility of any other authority, for example, the church, to judge the actions of the sovereign in the name of God. Following the original agreement, the sovereign was also granted the "right of judging the manner how God is to be honoured,"[190] therefore he holds absolute authority, without having to answer to the people or to those who think themselves to be the representatives of God on Earth. The main reason which determines Hobbes to make these statements is the desire to avoid having the sovereign's decisions questioned by a human authority which, by so doing, would place itself in a position of competition with the sovereign authority. At the same time, in order to avoid the risk of having the sovereign belief that he is entitled to decide whatever he wants, the idea of him answering to God must be admitted.

---

189 The expression is of Max Weber who has provided the definition of the state as "human community which (successfully) lays claim to the monopoly of legitimate physical violence within a certain territory, this 'territory' being another of the defining characteristics of the state." Max Weber, "The Profession and Vocation of Politics," in *Political Writings*, edited by Peter Lassman and Ronald Speirs (Cambridge: Cambridge University Press, 1994), pp. 310–311.

190 Hobbes, *De Cive*, chapter XV, § 17, pp. 195–196.

2.3.2 The reign of law and judiciary power

Those who deny the affinity between Hobbes and political liberalism insist on the fact that, when constituting civil society, individuals assign all their right to the sovereign; or, according to the liberal position, it is believed that individuals hold certain natural rights that any sovereign must observe, since they are inalienable. First, it may seem that from this perspective Hobbes is in opposition with political liberalism, but this is merely an appearance, since, according to his theory, individuals who leave the state of nature do not renounce their rights entirely. The reason why people agree to alienate their rights regards the insurance of peace and security; if this does not happen "no man is suppos'd to have submitted himselfe to ought, or to have quitted his Right to all things, before that there was a care had of his security."[191]

As we have seen, the state of nature is one of war of every one against every one and it lasts as long as the individuals do not decide to renounce some natural rights. These rights authorize them to do whatever they consider necessary in order to preserve their lives. By nature, each man has a tendency to accumulate as much power as possible and to limit the power of his adversaries. In order to put an end to this situation, individuals must renounce the use of their natural right over all things. Such a relinquishment is done to their benefit, since it allows the rational exercise of freedom, without the fear of being attacked at any given moment by their neighbors. This relinquishing is not efficient if the individuals do not grant the sovereign the absolute right to decide what the best means for peace and prosperity are. In this sense, only the sovereign can have the right to make laws and to instate public order. In the state which Hobbes has conceived, the subjects have alienated their political rights, meaning their right to decide concerning the way in which society is governed. Together with these rights, they have also alienated *the right to property*. Unlike Locke, for Hobbes such a right does not exist in the state of nature, since it cannot exist where there is no common power to guarantee possession of what individuals own. Property appears at the same time as the state and, moreover, it depends entirely on the state. When the sovereign is designated, he must carry out a partition of the goods of all his subjects, thus creating individual property. The sovereign distributes the goods and becomes the guarantor of this distribution, meaning that he warrants each subject the possibility of enjoying the goods that he has been allotted.[192] When distributing

191 Ibid., chapter VI, § 3, p. 93.

192 Hobbes, *Leviathan*, chapter XXIV, 5, p. 164 [127].

goods, the sovereign follows the principle of equity, meaning that his will is in accordance with natural equity.

The sovereign is the initiator of individual property through the civil laws that he makes, distributing the goods that in fact didn't belong to anyone at first, and which had virtually belonged to everyone. We can state that first these goods belonged to the communities, and then they entered into the jurisdiction of the sovereign. In Hobbes, collective property "is primary, individual property is nothing more than a way of motivating people in order to gain his own prosperity and that of the state."[193] For that matter, the property that a subject holds over his goods "consisteth in a right to exclude all other subjects from the use of them; and not to exclude their sovereign."[194] Since the sovereign has to be able to do all that he believes necessary for the survival of the political body, he must have the right to institute or to increase taxes and to dispose of the goods of his subjects. Therefore, it is obvious that if the right to property can be opposed between subjects, this cannot be the case where the sovereign is concerned. It is also the sovereign who settles the matter of means by which property can be transferred, given that "all kinds of contract between subjects, (as buying, selling, exchanging, borrowing, lending, letting, and taking to hire,) are to be made; and by what words and signs they shall be understood for valid."[195]

Regarding the means of acquiring wealth and therefore of growing one's property, Hobbes believes that there are four ways of doing so, namely: work[196], saving, gifts of nature and war[197]. However, the first two are the safest and the most important. As far as war is concerned, as a source for richness, the English philosopher points out that while it can be justified in the state of nature, it should not be taken into account in the civil state "because the art of war in regard to winnings is much like a game of chance, in which many lose their fortune and few make a profit."[198] Therefore, the sovereign must concern himself with the first three ways of getting rich. In order to do so, he must make laws which favor a better exploitation of the land and of the water, which discourage *faineance* and ensure what is needed for everyday life without too many expenses.

---

193 N. Campagna, *Thomas Hobbes. L'ordre et la liberté* (Paris : Michalon, 2000), p. 106.

194 Hobbes, *Leviathan*, chapter XXIV, 7, p. 165 [128].

195 Ibid., chapter XXIV, 10, p. 167 [130].

196 We note the importance that Hobbes grants to work, as the first factor of prosperity. In Locke, it will become a justifying factor for property.

197 Hobbes, *De Cive*, chapter XIII, § 14, p. 164.

198 Ibid.

If the sovereign wants to be powerful, he must make sure that his subjects prosper. The interest of the sovereign (considered as a moral person), the interest of every subject and general interest are all perfectly compatible. If the sovereign wishes his country to prosper, he must not exploit his subjects, nor should he instate an atmosphere of constant terror. If people live in fear, they do not have plans for the future, nor do they work in view of the future, since it appears to them as uncertain. In the state of nature, people led a miserable life, because no one could be certain that they could finally profit from the fruit of their labor and civil society was instituted precisely "that they might, as much as their humane condition would afford, live delightfully. They therefore who had undertaken the administration of power in such a kind of government (…) would to furnish their subjects abundantly, not only with the good things belonging to life, but also with those which advance to delectation."[199]

In the spirit of liberalism, Hobbes implicitly admits the idea that economic prosperity and the abuse of power cannot coexist. Contrary to liberal perceptions, he refuses however to impose constitutional limits on political power, but if he does so it is out of the conviction that the sovereign's understanding of the *raison d'Etat* is a strong enough reason to prevent the abuse of power. It is therefore necessary for the sovereign to understand that without insuring the prosperity of his country, he will not benefit from the necessary means to insure internal and external security or his own safety, which would make the danger of having the state of nature restored and the sovereignty lost.

In fact, the subjects have renounced those rights exercise of which would be susceptible of causing conflicts between them. Among these rights there is the right of not keeping promise and of subduing others when the preservation of life requires so; there is also the right to become the absolute master of all the goods that belong to others. Thus, in a certain manner, individuals have trade the right to wage war or to commit acts susceptible of leading to war – a right of absolute freedom – for the right of living in peace and security – a right of coercion.

In the chapter of the *Leviathan* dedicated to the freedom of subjects, Hobbes wonders what their true freedom actually is. A free man is defined as the one that "in those things, which by his strength and wit he is able to do, is not hindered to do what he has a will to."[200] Hence, the right to "freedom" is correlative to the need of security. Freedom coexists with fear since "generally all actions which men do in commonwealths, for fear of the law, are actions, which the doers had

199 Ibid., chapter XIII, § 4, p. 158.

200 Hobbes, *Leviathan*, chapter XXI, 2, p. 139 [108].

liberty to omit."[201] Also, freedom coexists with necessity since free actions come from the will of men, which is causally determined, the last cause being the will of God "the liberty of man in doing what he will, is accompanied with the necessity of doing that which God will, and no more, nor less."[202] In this way, we can say that since only the will of God is to be followed, man has the freedom to refuse the accomplishment of some actions, even if they are ordered by the sovereign. In order to ensure peace and the preservation of lives, men have created an artificial body, the political community. With it, they also created "artificial chains, called civil laws."[203] The subject's freedom can only be discussed by reference to these laws.

In order to answer the problem of the subject's freedom, Hobbes discusses the rights which people transfer in order to instate the sovereign power. He suggests two means of determining the obligations and the rights of subjects. One the one hand, there is a contract by means of which each individual accepts, together with the others, to transfer his rights to the sovereign authority. On the other hand, there is the objective for which the state was created, meaning the guarantee of having peace and security and the insurance of the each individual's right to rationally exercise his freedom. He admits that there is no political community with sufficient laws to regulate all the actions of men. As a result, they have the freedom to do what they rationally believe to be best for them, without losing sight of the purpose for which the state exists, namely to ensure peace and security. On the other hand, the laws have no power to protect individuals unless there is a person (or a group of persons) who has the ability to enforce their observance.

The act of submission to the sovereign power doesn't just imply the obligation, but also the freedom of subjects, since the act which institutes sovereign power also determines its limits. Some inalienable rights do exist, those that no rational being cannot and must not transfer. As a matter of fact, any transfer takes place in order to gain a personal advantage. In order to benefit from that advantage, the subjects need to be alive, which makes it very clear that they should not transfer their right to live through the agreement of not opposing those who wish to kill them. "If the sovereign command a man (though justly condemned,) to kill, wound, or maim himself; or not to resist those that assault him; or to abstain from the use of food, air, medicine, or any other thing, without which he

201 Ibid., chapter XXI, 3, p. 139 [108].
202 Ibid., chapter XXI, 4, p. 140 [108].
203 Ibid., chapter XXI, 5, p. 141 [109].

cannot live; yet hath that man the liberty to disobey."[204] Also, one must not transfer the right of being depraved of his freedom without resistance. The right to resist those who would kill or deprive the individual of his freedom is presented as an inalienable right and those who do not observe "they sin against the Lawes of Nature, (that is) against God."[205]

Just like we should always assume that the sovereign seeks equity, we must also assume that each individual's will is to lead a pleasant life, therefore none can be forced to agree to things which prevent the achievement of this purpose. The sovereign may command "and the Command may be such, as I would rather die then doe it; forasmuch therefore as no man can be bound to will being kill'd, much lesse is he tyed to that, which to him is worse then death."[206] In the state of nature, the perpetual threat means that the right to an agreeable life is being constantly violated. The institution of a sovereign power must warrant the observance of that right, and individuals mutually agree to obey such a power, with the express condition of having this right secured by that power. If the sovereign violates this right, people no longer have to obey it since, by violation of the inalienable rights of his subjects, the relationship between sovereign and subject became a relation of war between two individuals, namely a relation subject to natural laws[207]. If the sovereign is no longer able to protect his own people or no longer wishes to do so, the latter become once again a multitude in the state of nature, meaning that they rediscover their unlimited natural right and become their own protectors. By ceasing to protect his subjects, the sovereign restores the state of nature and will no longer enjoy any of the rights that had been transferred to him.

The above make it very clear that Thomas Hobbes admits the existence of inalienable rights, just like all liberal thinkers. However, there is a charge against his theory, namely the fact that he does not institutionalize these rights. He does not speak about limiting the sovereign's rights through law in any of his works. For Hobbes, the right to resist, far from being a positive one, remains a natural right. On the other hand, he rejects the idea of the oppressed people. As some writers have pointed out, his intention was not to turn power into a purpose of its own, but to turn it into more of a means. In his views, only a sovereign who hold absolute power is able to warrant each individual's freedom, meaning the freedom which does not infringe upon someone else's life, liberty or property.

204 Ibid., chapter XXI, 12, p. 145 [111–112]. ("Are not bound to hurt themselves").
205 Hobbes, *De Cive*, chapter VI, § 13, p. 98.
206 Ibid., chapter VI, § 13, p. 98.
207 Hobbes, *Leviathan*, chapter XXI, 21, p. 147 [114].

"The Leviathan holds absolute power in order to efficiently combat crime, not so that he may harass those who peacefully practice agriculture or commerce."[208]

Concerning the matter of negative freedom, that which is left to the free choice of men, its fields is not well defined yet. We learn that it is permitted by the sovereign and that it targets the freedom to buy, to sell, to conclude contracts, to set one's residence, to choose one's way of life and to educate one's children[209]. Still, as far as education is concerned, the sovereign has to be the one who decides what is taught in schools, especially in universities[210]. Here, Hobbes is faced with one of the most important issues of political theory, namely the clear definition of the limits to negative freedom. From this point of view, it is interesting to compare Hobbes position with that of Benjamin Constant, who states, in *Principes de politique*, concerning negative freedom, that "individuals should enjoy a complete freedom of action for all innocent or indifferent actions. As long as in a particular circumstance an action which is indifferent in itself can pose a threat for public safety, society has the right to forbid it… take for example, the gathering of some bandits before assassinating someone. Society has a right to intervene against this indifferent action, in order to prevent a crime. Society's intervention is legitimate since its necessity has been proven, but it is only legitimate with this condition"[211]. Society does not have the right to punish free association, but it does have the right as well as the duty to punish the guilty usage of this right. The crucial matter is to know who is qualified to establish what constitutes an innocent use and what constitutes a wrong use of freedom. As B. Constant points out, certain indifferent actions, meaning those innocent in themselves, can sometimes be wrong actions. One cannot define all the cases in which an innocent action becomes a wicked one. Therefore, there must be an authority who constantly keep a watch over the evolution of society and limits or abolishes certain freedoms, either because they pose a threat to the life, the freedom and the prosperity of others, either because their exercise leads to a weakening of the moral foundations of the state which is the warrant of the existence of negative freedoms. For B. Constant, this authority is civil society, for Hobbes it is the sovereign, which in fact represents society. For Constant, should the individual think that society has made abusive use of its rights against him, he may appeal to courts (actually, in B. Constant's theory, the state

208 Campagna, *Thomas Hobbes. L'ordre et la liberté,* p. 112.

209 Hobbes, *Leviathan*, chapter XXI, 6, p. 140 [109].

210 If universities were to teach the political theory of the ancient thinkers, some individuals might want to overthrow power.

211 Benjamin Constant, *Principes de Politique* (Paris: Hachette, 1997), p. 383.

is a constitutional one). In Hobbes, it might first seem that negative freedom is not protected from the whims of the sovereign, yet, as we shall see, in his theory courts play a pretty important part. Obviously, they are not independent from the will of the sovereign, yet they offer to the judges the right to watch over the observance of natural equity, which implies that all get what they deserve. Through the social contract, individuals have not transferred to the sovereign their right to forbid the exercise of negative freedom. Even if it is less protected, this does not stop us from associating Hobbes with the liberal tradition, since for him, the individual's submission to absolute power doesn't just represent an effective means of preventing the return to the state of nature, it is also the best guaranty offered to each individual, so that he may benefit from the rational exercise of his natural freedom.

Absolute power must guarantee subjects the possibility of exercising their freedom, but this is only possible if the sovereign uses his absolute power rationally. Through his actions, he must determine his subjects to understand that his sovereignty rights constitute the guarantee which allows them to exercise their freedom.

Often, the Leviathan is seen as a lawless state, in which the sovereign's will dictates everything, without the subjects having any judiciary guarantee. Basically, it is considered a despotic state. This image has contributed to the interpretation of Hobbes's theory of the state as a vanguard of the totalitarian doctrines of state expressed in the 20th century. However, a more objective reading of Hobbes's texts shows very clearly that the Leviathan is in fact a rule-of-law state, although it is not a constitutional state in the modern sense of the term.

According to the minimalist definition, a rule-of-law state is one in which law are in power. The rule of law is opposed to the government *de facto*[212], that is the rule of the blind force or of the self-will of the person who holds the power. In a rule of law political system, the power must be public; it must precisely define what is forbidden, it must be impartial both in content and in its enforcement, it must not be applied retroactively. Also, one necessary condition for the institution

212 The distinction between government "de jure" and government "de facto" was made by the Florentine Donato Giannotti (1492–1573) who "divided the whole history of law and politics into a battle between two parties: those fighting for the rule of law (or government 'de jure') and those fighting for the rule of certain particular men (or government 'de facto')", as related by Mortimer N. S. Sellers, "What Is the Rule of Law and Why Is It So Important?", in *The Legal Doctrines of the Rule of Law and the Legal State (Rechtsstaat)*, edited by James R. Silkenat, James E. Hickey Jr., Peter D. Barenboim (Dordrecht: Springer, 2014), p. 7.

of the reign of law is the respect of the citizens' rights. To that effect, we can state, without reserve, that Hobbes's Leviathan is definitely a reign of law.

In the state, in order for the laws to be effective, there have to be people who apply them. By reign of law it is understood that the laws do not govern by themselves: it is the sovereign who governs through these laws. If people were not animated by certain passions, they would simply follow the laws of nature and then we could say that the laws are in charge. But since this is not the way of things in real life, we have to report to a sovereign power in order to warrant, through force if need be, the observance of laws. These laws have been made in order to guarantee the observance of natural laws which are at the foundation of the state. Therefore, the civil laws encompass the natural law. The main function of civil laws consists in limiting the natural liberty of particular men, in such manner, as they might not hurt, but assist one another[213] with the purpose of warranting and extending peace. "For Hobbes, the civil law intervenes as a complex juridical system which must warrant the compulsory nature of its own norms, and it has the role of disciplining human actions."[214] As a written law, the civil law confirms the very principles of natural law; the civil law is therefore a good law, one which ensues from the moral bases of the natural law. It is also a useful law, since it regulates the relations between people. It is founded on the tangible power of sovereignty, which functions as an impersonal source of the legislative act.

Laws are necessary so that people know what is allowed and what is forbidden. It is only through laws that we can make the distinction between what is right and what is wrong. In the absence of this distinction, punishment makes no sense. A law is binding only if it is known. For this to happen, two conditions must be fulfilled. On the one hand, the laws have to be clear, on the other they have to be public, meaning that the subjects should have the opportunity to be informed about such laws. In this context, Hobbes makes reference to the laws of nature, which live in the hearts of all and are known by all; therefore, there is no need to have them written down or proclaimed.[215] No subject can stand on his ignorance concerning a law of nature and, for this reason, any breach of such laws constitutes a crime which the sovereign is entitled to punish.

Another element of the reign of law encountered in the *Leviathan* is that concerning the application of laws, which cannot be done retroactively. No law created

213 Hobbes, *Leviathan*, chapter XXVI, 8, p. 177, [139].

214 See Foisneau, *Politique, Droit et Théologie*, p. 23.

215 Hobbes, *Leviathan*, chapter XXVI, 8, p. 177 [138].

after the accomplishment of an act can identify that act as a criminal one, since "laws are the rules of just, and unjust; nothing being reputed unjust, that is not contrary to some law."[216] It follows that all that is not forbidden by law is permitted. An action which does not violate natural law can only be sanctioned when civil law forbids it. Also, civil law only applies to rational beings, the subjects who have the ability to rationally use their freedom, no matter their social standing, but "over natural fools, children, or madmen there is no law (…) nor are they capable of the title of just, or unjust; because they had never power to make any covenant or to understand the consequences thereof."[217] Any sanction must be preceded by a public condemnation, which in turn must be preceded by a trial, which has to be equitable and impartial, otherwise "for indignation carrieth men, not only against the actors, and authors of injustice; but against all power that is likely to protect"[218] the guilty. In other words, justice must be the same for everybody, no matter their social standing.

Although the sovereign has the right to make laws, to interpret them and to punish culprits, he is still bound by the laws of nature to follow certain rules in order to warrant the judiciary safety of his subjects. If these rules are not followed, none can have a secure future and there are no more differences between the natural and the social state. Therefore, the intention of abolishing the freedom of subjects cannot be originally attributed to Hobbes; the only legitimate objection would be that he did not want to institute constitutional guarantees against the sovereign. In the Hobbesian politic al regime, the reign of law is only protected by the good will of the sovereign. If he acts according to his interests, he will make sure that the minimal rules of the *legal state* are observed, but if he exercises his power as he well pleases, judiciary safety no longer exists and his subjects are entitled to believe that, once it is gone, their live and their freedom are once more in danger, just as in the state of nature.

Judiciary power is often thought of as a non-power. Like other theorists of law, Hobbes believes that the judge is a sort of machine who does nothing more than to apply the law by submitting a particular case to a general principle[219]. The fact that the judges can interpret the law while applying it is either ignored, either considered dangerous. To give judges the power to interpret the law is the equivalent of instituting what is called a "government by judges". In relation to legal questions, the *Leviathan* "with its important passage about the

216 Ibid., chapter XXVI, 4, p. 176 [137].
217 Ibid., chapter XXVI, 12, p. 179 [140].
218 Ibid., chapter XXX, 23, p. 231 [183].
219 See Campagna, *Thomas Hobbes*, p. 100.

interpretation of civil laws, can be chosen as a point of departure for a kind of new era."[220]

The issue of the politic role of judges only arises if we distinguish between the letter and the spirit (or the intent) of a law, meaning if we assume that a law only exists in the form of the interpretation given to it. This is what Hobbes does in the *Leviathan,* stating that "not the letter, (that is every construction of it,) but that which is according to the intention of the legislator, is the law."[221] Therefore, the essential matter which arises in relation to laws doesn't just concern who should issue them, it also concerns who is entitled to interpret them. Hobbes states that all laws, both the written and the unwritten ones, meaning civil but also natural laws should be interpreted."[222] This is the case for natural laws since some actions might break them, without being committed under the influence of passions. It is also the case for civil laws, which can easily be misinterpreted when words are given other meanings then their initial ones.

As far as the interpretation of laws in concerned, we have two possibilities: either everyone is entitled to interpret them, either this task falls to a body of experts. If we choose the first option, it means that we are going back to the state of nature, since each individual will be tempted to interpret the law as best suits him, thus making the existence of a common, universally valid law impossible, which makes the existence of the state impossible. Therefore, it is best to choose the second solution. Now all we need to do is to figure out whether the people who are qualified to interpret the law name themselves, or whether they are named by the sovereign. Hobbes's answer is very clear: only the sovereign has the right to establish who shall interpret the law.[223] The solution chosen by the English philosopher is motivated, again, by the fear of returning to the state of

---

220 Jean-Louis Halperin, "Legal Interpretation in 18th Century Europe: Doctrinal Debates Versus Political Change", in *Interpretation of Law in the Age of Enlightenment: From the Rule of the King to the Rule of Law*, edited by M. Yasutomo et al. (Dordrecht: Springer, 2011), p. 182.

221 Hobbes, *Leviathan*, chapter XXVI, 11, p. 179 [139].

222 The famous statement on interpretation concerns both types of law, written and unwritten, as Hobbes have been said: "All laws, written, and unwritten, have need of interpretation", Hobbes, *Leviathan*, chapter XXVI, 21, p. 183 [143].

223 "Hobbes recognized the sovereign's inability to make every interpretive and juridical decision alone. Thus, Hobbes legitimated the judicial right of interpretation as a product of delegation between social actors." Michael Stolleis, "Judicial Interpretation in Transition from the Ancien Régime to Constitutionalism", in *Interpretation of Law in the Age of Enlightenment: From the Rule of the King to the Rule of Law*, edited by M. Yasutomo et al. (Dordrecht: Springer, 2011), p. 4.

nature, since, if the task of interpreting the law belongs to a power which is not dependent on the sovereign's power, the two might come into conflict and again, the result might be civil war. Therefore, those who interpret the law, meaning the judges, should be named by the sovereign and they should only exercise this right in his name. Their decisions are backed up by the force of law, at least for the cases they are judging.

The formal distinction between the letter of the law and its intent doesn't tell anything about the matter of intention. In order to clarify this question, Hobbes introduces the notion of equity: "in the act of judicature, the judge doth no more but consider, whether the demand of the party, be consonant to natural reason, and equity; and the sentence he giveth, is therefore the interpretation of the law of nature; which interpretation is authentic; not because it is his private sentence; but because he giveth it by authority of the sovereign, whereby it becomes the sovereign's sentence; which is law for that time, to the parties pleading."[224] It follows that the judge's duty isn't just to decide whether a claim is justified or not, meaning if it is corresponds to positive laws or not. He must also decide if it is equitable or not, if it is in accordance with the laws of nature or not. The notion of equity requires that to each man should be given what rationally belongs to him. On the one hand, Hobbes states that it is the sovereign's will, and not reason which makes the law positive, but on the other hand he suggests that it is reason, and not the sovereign's will which creates equity. The judge must always assume that the sovereign desires equity and that is why he must interpret the sovereign's will (meaning the law) in a way that makes it compatible with equity. If, by applying the letter of the law he would reach a verdict which appears to him as being inequitable, it is his duty to make use of an interpretation in the spirit of the law.

Hobbes also admits that it might be possible for the sovereign to "err when judging equity"[225], without acting unjustly. The sovereign cannot act unjustly since his will is the foundation of positive law, defining what is just and what is unjust. However, his will may sometimes be inequitable, because equity is natural. Let's assume that the sovereign acts in a way which, although just, seems inequitable to a subject. The question which arises is if the latter is forced to accept the sovereign's decision. The answer is negative, since in the *Leviathan*, it is stated that, under certain conditions, the sovereign can be trialed. "If a subject have a controversy with his sovereign, of debt, or of right of possession of lands or goods, or

224 Hobbes, *Leviathan*, chapter XXVI, 23, p. 183, [143].
225 Ibid., chapter XXVI, 11, p. 179 [139].

concerning any service required at his hands, or concerning any penalty, corporal, or pecuniary, grounded on a precedent law; he hath the same liberty to sue for his right, as if it were against a subject; and before such judges, as are appointed by the sovereign."[226] Since they should rule according to the principles of equity, it is possible for a judge to interpret the law, meaning the sovereign's will, in the subject's favor. Of course, the sovereign who names the judges also has the right to revoke them. This is contrary to liberal tradition, which insists upon the impossibility of revoking judges, stating that it is the only means capable of warranting the independence of judicial power. Hobbes refuses this idea, fearing that if judges were independent from sovereign power, they might enter into conflict with the latter, thus causing civil war.

In Hobbes's conception, the role of the state is not that of creating or of promoting a more virtuous life, but to defend everyone's natural right. We can say that natural and civil law comprise one another. Positive law does not suppress natural law, but it translates it into practice. Natural laws, like that of equity, of justice and of gratitude take into account the merits which determine people to seek peace, and they only become actual laws in the context of the state. Just like natural law is a part of civil law in any organized state, civil law is also a part of natural law, provided that the observance of conventions and giving to each man what is his own are dictates of natural law. It follows that there are no major differences between natural and civil law, they are different aspects of law in general, one of which is unwritten, while the other is written. However, the right to natural freedom can be restricted by civil laws, because the purpose of making laws is to enforce such restrictions in the absence of which peace cannot exist, and the law was created precisely in order to limit the natural freedom of men so that they are unable to harm one another, but to help one another and to unite against a common enemy. The condition which makes the existence of rational (therefore peaceful) action possible is the absolute power of the sovereign. The sovereign's competence in the social state has the broadness and the characteristics of the competence of natural law in the state of nature. The sovereign's absolute power is the echo of the unrestricting natural law[227]. Thus, to say that the sovereign is all powerful because he alone keeps his rights from the state of nature equals saying that only he keeps the competence of those rights, for he embodies necessity, the source of rights in this state and also the possibility of overcoming this state.

---

226 Ibid., chapter XXI, 19, p. 146, [113].

227 Manent, *Naissance de la politique moderne*, Deuxième partie: «Hobbes», Chapitre I [consulted in Romanian translation, p. 80].

Therefore, we can see that in Hobbes's works, all the laws which lead to the instatement of civil society are ensued from the concept of human nature. As result, in the hobbesian doctrine, "human nature" is not just a descriptive and explanatory concept; first of all it is a boundary concept. The state of nature is not just the initial state, the one which proceeds society, it also pertains to the definition of humanity; it is the danger that constantly threatens humanity and follows it from the shadows. At the same time, it is the principle of any virtue.

Chapter 3: Hobbes's theory of obligation

The transfer of rights through the social contract creates the political obligation of the subjects towards the sovereign. It is only by acknowledging his authority that people can hope to avoid the permanent threat of a violent death determined by the continuous desire of gaining power over others, this desire being characteristic of human nature. Thus, political obligation is inferred from human nature, which, according to Hobbes, is a moral obligation. People acknowledge their obligation towards the sovereign because this is in their own best interest. The matter which arises here actually aims at the fact that, from the perspective of classic morals, an obligation which is based exclusively on one's own interest cannot be considered as moral (at most, it is prudent). A true moral obligation must be based on something that goes beyond the limits of one's own interest. Obviously, for Hobbes, the issue is not discussed in these terms. The value of an obligation (which consists in its capacity to bind) can only be tested in practice. Or, practice hasn't shown that an obligation which is based on something beyond one's own interest binds people more firmly and to a greater extent than the latter. Moreover, Hobbes considers that "the new type of obligation is more efficient and bounded of men needs and capacities."[228] The obligation to which he is referring is based not only on his own interest, but also on something less noble, like fear. For this consideration, Hobbes was considered by the historians of ideas as a legal positivist.[229] However, it is equally based on reason. It is more moral for people to justify their actions through their own reason than to evoke distant essences or divinities.

In Hobbes's works, morality is discussed from the moment when he infers the equality of rights from the equality of faculties and of purposes. Since in

228 Macpherson, *The Political Theory of Possessive Individualism*, p. 73.

229 "Strictly speaking, it is, of course, anachronistic to speak of Hobbes as a legal positivist. [...] Nonetheless, many philosophers have been struck by the evident affinities between Hobbes's views on civil law and those of Austin and Bentham, Kelsen and Hart." Lloyd, *Morality in the Philosophy of Thomas Hobbes: Cases in the Law of Nature*, p. 264. David Dyzenhaus has argued against "the orthodox understanding of Hobbes as an early legal positivist," David Dyzenhaus, "Hobbes on the authority of law", in *Hobbes and the Law*, edited by David Dyzenhaus and Thomas Poole (Cambridge: Cambridge University Press, 2012), p. 194. He said that Hobbes is not an early legal positivist, nor a predecessor of H.L.A. Hart, since "Hobbes advances a theory of legal authority in which the 'laws of nature' are given a prominent role in the determination of the content of the law". Ibid., p. 188.

the state of nature all men are equal, there is no reason why they shouldn't have the same rights. The transfer of these rights gives rise to the political obligation which Hobbes assimilates into moral obligation, since it is derived from the transfer of rights which are considered moral. The novelty brought in by Hobbes is that he believes rights and obligations to be derived directly from facts (meaning from natural equality), while in moral philosophy, starting with Plato, rights and obligations have been inferred from the capacities and the will of men, in an indirect manner. More to the point, the capacities and the will of men have been considered as effects of the purposes of nature and of divine will, the latter being considered the first cause of the capacities and the desires of men, and also, as the source of rights and of moral obligations. This aspect differs from one philosopher to another, depending on the purposes and on the will that are attributed to God (therefore to an exterior force) and, in general, they are not the same for all men. Hobbes thinks of rights and obligations as being comprised in every individual's need to survive. All men are entitled to self-preservation; in their quality of rational beings they have the capacity to obey the rules which insure this right.

The equality of abilities and of purposes in the state of nature doesn't just result in equal insecurity; it also results in the equal need for a system of political obligation. Therefore, it is obvious that an external system of values cannot be imposed. For this reason, there is no question of establishing a hierarchy of desires, of rights or of obligations. All men must be considered equal, and this equality constitutes a sufficient source of rights and obligations: "Hobbes was the first philosopher who deduced the rights and obligations from facts without putting anything unreal into the facts. This is his revolution in the political and moral philosophy."[230]

The essential condition for the existence of a system of compulsoriness, be it a moral or a political one, is for people to believe that their equality targets more important aspects than inequality. This is the only way of making sure that no one can expect to be considered superior to others. If equality were not admitted, some people might claim unlimited rights and then any moral obligation would be impossible. Hobbes understood this and, as we have shown, he has argued, from the perspective of the postulate of equality, that there is no reason why some should have more than others, which ensues the possibility and the necessity of moral and political obligation.

230 Macpherson, *The Political Theory of Possessive Individualism*, p. 78.

3.1 The critique of Hobbesian theory by John Locke

Leo Strauss pointed out that Hobbes's greatest merit was that of asserting, contradicting Machiavelli, that the subordination of all the individual interests to the "reason of state" is not legitimate and that the only legitimate "reason of state" is the insurance of the individual's rights and security: "The 'reason of state' school replaced 'the best regime' by 'efficient government.' The 'natural public law' school replaced 'the best regime' by 'legitimate government.'"[231] According to the previously quoted author, the theories on "natural public law" are in search of a social order that can be legitimated no matter the circumstances. The idea of the best form of government is abandoned and instead, we will find the idea of a right order that will have to give a universal solution to the political issue. This solution will be seen in close connection with the obligation concerning the political issue and its relation to moral obligation.

In this context it can be said that Thomas Hobbes was the first thinker who achieved a theoretical exposition of the real principles that must underlie civil government. Just like Grotius or Pufendorf, he established that the origin of civil society lies in a certain state of nature which precedes it. John Locke will broadly start from the same hypothesis, maintaining the essential distinction between the natural and the civil state, but he will also attempt to justify it. In an attempt to bring a few specifications to the meaning of the concept of *state of nature of mankind*, Locke formulated the first important criticism of Hobbes's doctrine.

The author of the *Two treatises about government* noticed a number of aspects to which the hobbesian theory of the state of nature did not pay enough attention. Thereby, concerning the question of how long does human existence last in a state of nature, Locke answers that it lasts until the shaping of the common political society, but this does not mean that the state of nature ends once different societies are formed. For Locke, it is obvious that overcoming the state of nature is not achieved by creating a universal state that includes all of mankind. Rather, people formed small communities or independent states linked by natural or civil relations. Thus, the self-sufficient states are in a state of nature as long as there are no laws to regulate their relations, except the natural law or the law of the strongest. Even allied, the sovereign states maintain between them a state of nature as long as there is no certain common convention to end it. Moreover, Locke insists that not all contracts put an end to the state

231 Strauss, *Natural Right and History*, p. 191. Strauss used the expression "natural public law" in order to set apart the political theories of Thomas Hobbes and of John Locke from the school of natural right (represented by Grotius or by Pufendorf).

of nature; this is merely the case for common agreements to join a community and to form a political body. People can make promises and contracts without putting an end to the state of nature by doing these. For example, a Swiss and an Indian who meet in the American Forests can close some conventions without entering a political society. These conventions must be, without a doubt, respected, because the truth and the faith are natural obligations[232], but their compliance does not put to the issue nor destroys the state of nature. People will remain in the state of nature up until when, by their own will, they will become members of a political society.

Therefore, the state of nature is the relationship between people by virtue of their human nature, irrespective of all the relationships in civil society. Along this line, the state of nature will always exist, because all people are firstly humans, before being the citizens of a state. The state of nature is not one of wilderness, in which people obey only the law of the strongest and their own needs, it is a state in which, even in the absence of civil and political laws, a law still exists, namely the natural law. This law precedes and surpasses all social laws, it commands individual passions and it is compulsory for all people. The precedence of the state of nature must not be interpreted only chronologically, although it is clear that it is *also set in time* before any civil convention, this being valid for every single individual (who is first of all human and only then a citizen). This point of view would be simply strictly historical and would lead the discussion about the state of nature on a ground that Locke wishes to avoid, because of the numerous difficulties it would raise. According to a number of authors, Locke uses the concept of state of nature more in the rational and moral acceptation than in the historical one. For Locke, natural law is the one which ensures that people benefit from the four fundamental rights preceding any civil society, namely the right to life, to health, to freedom and to property[233]. But if Locke imagines the state of nature in this manner it is because he tries to solve a difficulty that Hobbes's doctrine raises. We saw that, according to the author of the *Leviathan*, the state of nature is one of war, a war of every one against every one, and what causes the people's urge to create civil and then political communities is the fear of death. The problem that now raises is whether, in the hobbesian concept of state of nature, the individual as such is defined in an acceptable manner. The answer that one can

232 Locke, *Two Treatises of Government*, p. 277. [Second Treatise, II, 14].

233 Under the influence of these ideas, Thomas Jefferson pointed out, in the *Declaration of independence of the United States of America*, written in 1776, that the inalienable rights of men are the right to life, the right to freedom and the right to aspire to happiness.

foresee in Hobbes's *Leviathan* is negative, because, according to him, the human individual does not possess anything of his own except the fear of death and the obsessive desire for self-preservation. The human being defines itself as an individual only in relation to the hostility of others and to their strategies to kill him, strategies that he has to thwart. This can lead to the apparently strange conclusion that "individuals in the state of nature are not truly individuals entitled to rights intrinsically belonging to them."[234] Therefore, Locke's political philosophy project consists in the attempt to "interpret the individual in his state of nature, in order to associate inherent rights to him", as Pierre Manent says. The state of nature is the one in which people do not kill, do not harm themselves, keep their promises and respect the ones with whom they come into contact. Even if in this state the individual is absolutely free, he is not free of duties towards others, by complying with the natural law and all its precepts. For this reason, unlike Hobbes, Locke must reckon that the state of nature is one of peace and good cohabitation, and not one of war against everyone else.

Therefore, the state of nature is mainly characterized by the fact that it is a state of absolute freedom and equality in which people have the possibility "to order their actions and dispose of their possessions and persons, as they think fit, [...] without asking leave, or depending upon the will of any other man."[235] Surely this happens only within natural law, because the state of freedom does not mean a state of absolute tolerance. Even if the human being has the boundless freedom to dispose of his own person and property, he does not have the freedom to destroy himself, nor to destroy other living beings in his possession, except when there is a higher goal than his own preservation. Also, as a state of equality, the state of nature implies that "all the power and jurisdiction is reciprocal, no one having more than another."[236] One more likely deals with an equality of law than with one of fact, because it refers to equal moral dignity, to the identity of abilities and of needs. The "great maxims of justice and charity"[237] derive from this natural equality. Given the fact that in the state of nature all humans are free and equal, it turns out that there is no such thing as the right of natural domination of one man over another. Moreover, a man's first duty is to preserve his life, because nobody has the right to destroy his own life. This right, that the individual does not have, cannot be given to another, so

234 Pierre Manent, *An Intellectual History of Liberalism* (Princeton: Princeton University Press) 1996. p. 40.

235 Locke, *Two Treatises of Government*, p. 269. [Second Treatise, II, 4].

236 Ibid., p. 269. [Second Treatise, II, 4].

237 Ibid., p. 270. [Second Treatise, II, 5].

the individual cannot renounce his natural freedom, the guarantee of his own preservation.[238]

Therefore Locke amends the hobbesian doctrine, considering that the state of nature is not one of war, because, if it were so, one should say that "what is the most natural thing in that natural condition of mankind is not the independent individual as such, it is the war of all against all that gives him birth."[239] In other words, the individual would enter society without anything of his own and, once the peace of the Leviathan is established, he should continue the state of nature in some manner, through hostile relations to define his individuality. This actually means that the hobbesian way of considering the legitimacy of political power can engender some difficulties. That is exactly why Locke finds himself in a position to consider the state of nature as a peaceful coexistence of all individuals. However, "Locke begins like Hobbes: the first need and therefore man's fundamental right is that of self-preservation."[240] However, this concept no longer refers to the hostility of others, but to the need of ensuring subsistence conditions. The behavior of natural man is animated by hunger and by the need to satisfy it.

In a state of nature, satisfying this need implies a minimal effort, like gathering the fruits of the earth, or a more consistent effort, like the cultivation of land. The most important thing is that this effort means work and that its results enter directly in the individual's possession. The constitution of the individual as such is not achieved by relation to the hostility of others, nor through the isolation dictated by the uncertainty of the cohabitation in the same space, but through the fact that the acute need to ensure one's subsistence implies relating to oneself without suffering from the hobbesian persecution mania. "The right [to eat] is thus independent of any consent"[241]. According to Pierre Manent, Locke would carry on a simplification of Hobbes's doctrine. In the *Leviathan*, the reason for the war of every one against every one was the will for power, pride and the blind and natural need to dominate others. Things are simpler for Locke: in the state of

238 Locke admits two exceptions to this principle, namely, when dealing with a power exercised over a criminal or over a prisoner of war. In these cases, he believed, the master's absolute power must be acknowledged, beyond any convention. According to some critics, this concession is, however, "imprudent, since this right of war is what jurisprudents fundament slavery on." Janet, *Histore de la science politique*, vol. II, p. 208.

239 Manent, *An Intellectual History of Liberalism*, p. 40.

240 Ibid., p. 40.

241 Ibid., p. 42.

nature, people pursue the satisfaction of their subsistence needs. Even so, Locke's theory cannot escape the "hobbesian moment". The state of nature cannot be maintained continuously, because people are not always rational and therefore, the order dictated by reason is disturbed by passions. The strong and violent men claim to have all the goods for themselves, threatening the property of others, their freedom and even their life. In any case, it is only now that the state of nature turns into a state of war, exactly because people do not comply anymore with the state of nature. In this state of war, natural law gives everyone the right to defend oneself and to punish others. Thus, every individual has the right to call to account those who defy the natural law and who, by so doing, place themselves in the position of enemies of mankind.

The situation presented above entitles us and other commentators to believe that "although the [lockean] state of nature is not a state of war, it tends naturally to become so."[242] The simplification of Hobbes's doctrine would consist in the fact that, for Locke, the state of nature is not by definition one of war, because violence and revenge do not belong to the human nature, but becomes in the end a *de facto* state of war. The difference seems to reside only in the nuance: "any doctrine of the state of nature and the social contract (even Rousseau) necessarily has a Hobbesian moment."[243] However, as a consequence of this "nuance", a fall will later gape between Hobbes and Rousseau concerning the definition of human nature and the justification of political order, but also between Locke and Rousseau, since Rousseau will blame everything about property. The question is now if property and individual's desire to own more can give a satisfactory explanation for the evolution of lockean humanity from the natural happiness to "the hobbesian moment" of war.

In his *Essays on the Laws of nature*, Locke continues Hobbes's distinction between natural right, which – as a right – refers to the freedom of doing something or not and (natural) law, which refers to interdiction. The issue which arises is that, since we distinguish between right and law, we are forced to submit right to law and to limit it by law. When Hobbes stated that where there is no law there is no injustice, he was referring to the civil laws which establish what is wrong and what is right, what is just and what is unjust, without any reference to natural law, while according to Cicero and to Locke, human laws by themselves can only be considered good or bad by comparison to natural law.

242 Ibid., p. 48.
243 Ibid., p. 48.

We have shown that Hobbes infers the natural law from the fear of a violent death, the strongest passion and most fundamental of all natural aspirations. Death is seen by Hobbes as nature's greatest enemy, therefore the fear of death is a natural attitude that surpasses all other instincts and desires, being their "reason" itself. In Hobbes, passions are not in contradiction of principle with reason, given the fact that, by virtue of his systematic materialism, he conceives reason as not being determined by transcendent principles. Reason is a simple calculation of the means that can ensure self-preservation (which was interpreted as atheism and political hedonism)[244]. Therefore, the possibility of the social contract as rational enterprise is already presumed in the realism of passions, whereas people can understand, through right reason, that the necessity to secure self-preservation requires postponing all other natural impulses, for an indeterminate time. Only a power, greater than all other powers, can guarantee the observance of this limitation.

The fact of putting the principle of self-preservation at the base of the social contract has the following meaning for Hobbes: "the fundamental moral fact is not a duty but a right; all duties are derivative from the fundamental and inalienable right of self-preservation. There are, then, no absolute or unconditional duties [...] Only the right of self-preservation is unconditional or absolute. [...] The law of nature, which formulates man's natural duties, is not a law, properly speaking."[245] Hence, it turns out that the birth of the state is a necessity and its role is not that of achieving virtue, like in Aristotle's political theory, but that of ensuring the individual's natural right. Taking this as a starting point, Leo Strauss reaches the conclusion that the founder of liberalism is Hobbes, as long as by liberalism we understand "that political doctrine which regards as the fundamental political fact the rights, as distinguished from the duties, of man and which identifies the function of the state with the protection or the safeguarding of those rights."[246] The foundation of political ethics on the problem of rights and not on the problem of obligations is the direct consequence of individualism.

As shown by Leo Strauss, prior to [Hobbes], the term "state of nature" was at home in Christian theology rather than in political philosophy. "The state of

---

244 In order to make the phrase "political hedonism" understandable, Leo Strauss offers the example of a quote from Burke (*Letter to Rivarol*, June 1st 1791): "The Parisian philosophers ... explode or render odious or contemptible, that class of virtues which restrain the appetite. ... In the place of all this, they substitute a virtue which they call humanity or benevolence." Strauss, *Natural Right and History*, p. 188.

245 Ibid., p. 181.

246 Ibid., p. 181–182.

nature was distinguished especially from the state of grace, and it was subdivided into the state of pure nature and the state of fallen nature."[247] The hobbesian state of nature has an anti-theological significance,[248] whereas Locke will restore the theological distinction between the *genuine* state of nature and the *fallen* state of nature. Right in middle of the puritan revolution and of the exacerbation of religious sensitivity, the author of the *Treaty* will reject the hobbesian theory of the state of nature as a *pure hypothesis*.

In the works of Locke, the *effective* character of the state of nature is still to be clarified, following two accepted views of the state of nature: a primordial state of nature and a secondary state of nature. The secondary state of nature is the state of war, and its significance is identical to Hobbes's unique state of nature. As for the primordial state of nature, this one seems by far more hypothetical even than Hobbes's hypothesis. Since it admits that the natural state of war, which is primordial for Hobbes and secondary for Locke, is actually the generalization of a *de facto* behavior, the hobbesian hypothesis consists of accepting this fact as natural and primordial one. For Locke, on the contrary, this fact is not sufficient and he assumes that, beyond this nature, there is *another* nature that could explain *why* the people in the state of war are drawn towards the social contract.

The disagreement concerning the state of nature is nothing more than a concealed dispute regarding the best or the worst form of government. Locke considers that the hobbesian state of nature is hypothetical because, if human nature is "bad", then any form of government is better than the state of nature, and absolute monarchy would prove to be the best. In order to reject this conclusion, Locke assumes that the state of war cannot be that bad, in any case not worse than absolute monarchy, as it is a *derivative* state of nature. The natural state of war is not to be mistaken for human nature; the latter is a good one in the original situation, although it is actually evil in the fallen situation. The opposition between Hobbes and Locke boils down to the opposition between two metaphysical hypotheses. Locke has on his side the common sense and the Christian tradition, while Hobbes shares the materialist belief of the mechanistic philosophy of nature from which he derives a moral skepticism.

---

247 Ibid., p. 188.

248 Although Hobbes was "a sincere and believing Christian," [...] "we must interpret his Christianity so that it is not incompatible with the secular structure and content of his moral and political conception. In conclusion, the whole order of Hobbes's exposition seems to imply that the secular structure and content of his doctrine is regarded by him as basic." Rawls, *Lectures on the History of Political Philosophy*, pp. 38–39.

The actual significance of the modern theories of social contract is no longer given by the problem of the best form of government. From this point of view, both Hobbes's and Locke's theories concern the history of political philosophies. But we believe that these theories still have enough resources along the lines of the relation between morals and politics, which means that they have to be regarded as a dialogue in which, beyond doctrinal opposition, one can spot a certain number of common assumptions. In that sense, we have to point out that the idea of a "good" nature in Locke does not imply the fact that man, ever since the state of nature, is capable of perceiving and of hating Evil and Injustice, in the sense that he would possess a certain number of innate and eternal virtues.

This way of understanding the problem is not very suited to the modern theory of the natural right, as it implies a prior theory of virtue, much like in classical tradition. The natural law theory does not explain for example if the individual has an innate knowledge of good and evil, of truth and lies, although it has to be able to extract all these values from the principle of natural reason. Hobbes and Locke are in perfect agreement with regard to this aspect. "Good" and "Evil" are understood in the sense of utilitarianism, as the presence or the absence of pleasure or pain: "good" is what contributes to self-preservation (broadly, as satisfaction of desires and unlimited growth of power), and "evil" is what prevents it. Locke's idea that man, in the state of nature, has the tendency to limitlessly purchase properties is the perfect equivalent of Hobbes's idea of every individual's tendency to infinitely increase his power.

From this point of view, we believe that the opinion according to which the idea of property is not present in Hobbes is absolutely false. The definition of "the power of a man"[249] as totality of the means to acquire a present or future good is actually the definition of property. It is exactly this equivalence between property and power that will determine the understanding of the sovereign's power as the exertion of a property right over the civil society – *the dominion*[250] – and

249 Hobbes, *Leviathan*, chapter X, 1, p. 58 [41].

250 In the *Leviathan,* Hobbes will name "Of Commonwealth" the second part, which discusses the issue of sovereignty and will use the term "dominion" only in the chapter about paternal dominion ("Of Dominion Paternal, and Despotic"). If we take into account that for Hobbes, sovereignty through acquirement and through conquest is yet another form of contract, since it involves the consent ("not by victory, but by the consent of the vanquished"), we may might postulate that any commonwealth in which there is an absolute monarchy is in fact a *dominion paternal, and despotic* (at least this I show John Locke sees the matter). As proof, in *De Cive*,

will draw Locke's criticism of absolutism. Also, for the same reason, Locke will feel forced to conceive a labor theory. Labor is what allows the individual to sell himself as a slave, but also to set himself free, in the sense that he is no longer the sovereign's property, but he belongs to himself, together with whatever he produces. The idea of production is intended to limit the sovereignty theory, as the sovereign cannot own a good that does not exist at the moment of the "signing" of the contract. Even if the land would entirely belong to him, he could not own work, therefore, he could not own the "secret" of producing wealth and happiness. But this separation introduced by Locke does not affect in anything the understanding of Hobbes's idea that the natural individual has the tendency to limitlessly increase his power. When saying that Hobbes's natural man is "evil" and that of Locke's is "good" one only refers to the psychology of the relation of sociability, in other words, to the "hostile" or "gentle" behavior of the human animal.

This difference of perspective becomes meaningful only in reference to the observation that natural law would not be a law unless it would provide sanctions and unless natural individuals would be capable of applying these sanctions. Every individual is both judge and executor of the natural law. If man is conceived in accordance with Hobbes's model, this demand is carried out through the right of war. If man is to be thought according to Locke's theory, it is the right of peace which takes priority, since in the state of nature every man is a justice of the peace. But the sanction of natural law in the natural law of peace is not given by the judgment of conscience: "conscience is nothing else but our own opinion or judgment of the moral rectitude or pravity of our own actions."[251] While Hobbes's theory was for the most part a simplifying one, in return, Hobbes did not need a speculation about primitive history: from a Hobbesian point of view, the caveman in his wild state and the man of the 20th century in the middle of civil war, have in common the same natural condition. In fact, from here, one could understand Hobbes's theory about the state of nature as a *pure* hypothesis (possibly having a *polemic* extent, as Leo Strauss states in a debate)[252]. Our opinion is that this point of view is nevertheless inaccurate; it ensues from

Hobbes entitles *Dominion* the part which discusses sovereignty and which in the *Leviathan* will be called "Of Commonwealth".

251 Strauss, *Natural Right and History*, p. 222.

252 Leo Strauss, "Notes on Carl Schmitt, 'The Concept of the Political'" in *The Concept of the political*, by Carl Schmitt, translated and with an Introduction by George Schwab, with a Foreword by Tracy B. Strong, and Notes by Leo Strauss, 99–122 (Chicago and London: The University of Chicago Press, 2007).

the fact that an exaggerate importance is given to the systematic and deductive aspect of the *Leviathan*. At the time, civil war was proving to Hobbes that this "hypothesis" generates disastrous effects. It is true though that, in Hobbes, time does not affect humanity's natural condition, as Locke believed. If, in *The Second Treaty*, the state of nature is presented like a sort of history, this is because Locke needs both hypotheses: the one of the "good" man and the one of the "bad" man. In order not to contradict himself from a logical point of view, he has to think of man's goodness and of man's malice in a temporal succession.

Therefore Locke takes as a starting point Hobbes's natural state of war and turns it into an intermediate state between a "natural society" presumed as native, and a "conventional society" established through the social contract. In relation to Hobbes, Locke will need to take a step back in order to be able to take a step forward. In order to introduce the legitimate civil war (the revolution) into the society, first, one needs to introduce society into the state of nature. The right to war had to be preceded by the right to peace, and the right to peace is a right of conventions and of property. This is why the "contradictions" that are blamed on Locke are actually consequences of some postulates that the English philosopher introduces in addition to the axioms of *actual state of nature*.

By this *actual* state of nature we understand the very state of nature described by Hobbes, namely the state of war that *generates*, by virtue of the self-preservation principle, the social contract. As shown above, all the doctrines of the state of nature had to concede a "hobbesian moment" synonymous with the war of every one against every one. The natural state of war which leads to the emergence of society is an *effective* one, while the state of nature which corresponds to the initial state of man is a *hypothetical* one. The simplification of the premises in Hobbes consists in the identification of the former with the latter, in the sense that the state of war is the very expression of the human nature, while in Locke the state of war is the fall of man. For Locke, the natural condition of mankind is twofold: first one of equality, then one of inequality; first a primitive one, then a derivative one; first a social one, then a natural one. Locke will consider Hobbes's state of nature as only *hypothetical*, because it does not generate sanctions. For him, the state of nature is effective only if natural law has a direct influence over men. In principle, this point of view is correct. But a state of nature which would be firstly a state of peace and secondly a state of effectiveness of the natural law is a supposition that cannot be verified by any fact; therefore the effective character of the natural law is also a pure hypothesis. Paradoxically, it is through the Hobbesian state of war that the natural law can be thought as having effects, since the state of war leads to the formation of society without being in contradiction with natural law. Yet it is not obvious in what way one can consider, in Hobbes, that the natural law could generate sanctions, as Locke requires. This is why the Hobbesian state of nature appears to be a "hypothetical" one. However, if the natural law is effective through the state of war (since the war leads to the emergence of society), then isn't positive right itself a sanction which the natural law applies?[253]

Here lies the apple of discord: to conceive positive right as a sanction of the natural law against human nature means to justify absolutism as the safest means by which natural law is instated into its rights. This is why Locke cannot accept the idea that the state of nature is real in Hobbes doctrine; it is a *flatus vocis*. Hobbes considers absolutism as a sanction of human nature. On the contrary, Locke considers the (English) civil war as a legitimate sanction of absolutism. But if revolution must overthrow tyranny, then it must maintain and guarantee property. Property is the central point of Locke's theory; it outlives the natural state of war, the positive right and the civil war. Locke gives (too) much importance to property and freedom in order to be able to consider their foundations without contradiction. This is why Leo Strauss used to say that modern political philosophy is not possible without doctrine. This clarification will allow us to understand that, beyond the political consequences that belong to the legitimacy of some form of government or another, the outlook on human nature creates a different opinion concerning the relation between political duty and moral duty.

3.2 A liberal interpretation of Hobbes

Hobbes's traditional interpreters put together his theory of political obligation starting from two theses: a) the hobbesian theory of human physiology considers the man outside of any social relation; b) this theory contains enough elements to infer from it the necessity of a sovereign state. According to Crawford Brough Macpherson[254] the two theses are "abusive simplifications", as the necessity of a political order could not follow from concerns regarding desires, imagination, memory or other faculties, in the absence of a series of assumptions concerning the individual's behavior in relation with other people. Such an example – Macpherson says – is Hobbes's assertion that people show signs of an unlimited tendency to increase their power in spite of others. Concerning the relations

253 John Rawls noted that, given the purpose of legitimizing an existing effective Sovereign, the state of nature in Hobbes must be interpreted as hypothetical: "for this purpose, the hypothetical interpretation does seem to suffice." Rawls, *Lectures on History of Political Philosophy*, p. 34.

254 C.B. Macpherson, *The Political Theory of Possessive Individualism: Hobbes to Locke* (Oxford and New York: Oxford University Press, 1962).

between men, the paragraph in question[255] already implies that humans in the state of nature possess some features that rather belong to civilized men living in society. We saw how this difficulty was noted by Locke, who believed in the necessity to imagine natural man as possessing some features of his own, some rights, ever since the state of nature. Locke therefore defines the human individual in a way that justifies the conduct of the citizen as an *owner*: the institution of property – as possession of goods – is anterior to the civil state, he says. The question is whether Hobbes might have done the same, nevertheless by adjusting the premises so that the citizen would be deprived of the right to rebellion.

It is obvious, according to Macpherson, that Hobbes's theory about the psychology and physiology of man is not sufficient, to explain how natural man passed from the state of nature to the establishment of the civil state; in order to do this, the postulate of sociability would be needed. If it would be question about people living in small communities and manifesting the same type of behavior, then the Hobbesian mechanistic theory could explain the establishment of the state and could legitimate the submission to the sovereign. Locke, who admits sociability, will solve this problem in two steps, as we saw earlier. Hobbes – who does not admit sociability, will make a series of implicit observations and descriptions which will point in that direction, but at the expense of an ambiguous concept of the state of nature. Macpherson believes that when Hobbes thought of state of nature as a premise of the absolutist state, he previously included in the definition of human nature a series of elements which rather pertain to social behavior. Therefore, the concept of state of nature is ambiguous in Hobbes.

Before looking at Macpherson's arguments, we first analyze independently the possibility of a double meaning of Hobbes's state of nature. This allows us to place Macpherson's interpretation in a broader context. Concerning Hobbes's concept of state of nature we have noticed that it was inherited from the philosophical tradition. As shown by Leo Strauss, Hobbes is the first modern philosopher who gave a completely new significance to the idea of state of nature and of natural law. As we showed in the first chapter, the pagan philosophers conceived the state of nature in accordance with the true nature of man, while the scholastic philosophers or those belonging to the school of natural law have referred to natural state as being in harmony with the Christian theology. Hobbes's innovation consists in the reversal of the moral philosophies' problem by stating that the idea of state of nature leads to the question of legitimate government, and not to the one of "good" government as before. For the first time, political theory was

255 Hobbes, *Leviathan*, chapter XI, 1, p. 65 [47].

not preceded by a theory of virtue and of moral obligation. This revolution was made possible forasmuch Hobbes starts from a theory of human nature that was built on empirical observations, like the description of human relations during civil war. So even if the theory of human nature is presented as a logical hypothesis, as shown by the best part of Hobbes's interpreters, it is understood that the "observation of facts" idea suggests the foundation of society as an *effect* of this nature, such as one can observe in the case of the civil war, when people end up settling for any form of government instead of anarchy.

Hobbes's doctrine of necessity, present in his theory of human nature as well as in his natural philosophy, implies the idea of chaining causes and effects, hence a temporal succession. Here is the reason why, even if Hobbes's theory of the state of nature is not historical (since Hobbes does not speak of the original or of the primitive man), he still consider, in *De Cive*, that "the naturall state of men, before they entr'd into Society, was a meer War, and that not simply, but a War of all men, against all men."[256] This acknowledgement of the state of nature as a temporal duration seems improper for the Hobbesian doctrine, since it gives somebody to understand that, as in the case of Locke's and Rousseau's doctrines, the social contract should mark a definitive break with primitivism and savagery. "State of nature" in the historical sense would mean that, even if it would happen that, from time to time, the social bond be broken – which it actually occurs quite often, like shown by Hobbes – the man would be unable to return to his previous state, because of the changes that social life has brought about in his inner life.[257] Or, the civil war has showed to Hobbes and to everybody that human nature does not change, so there is no "historical sense"! Nevertheless one must admit that, even if not in *Leviathan*, the historical meaning – and this is the first meaning – of the state of nature is not completely unfamiliar to Hobbes.

---

256 Hobbes, *De Cive,* chapter I, § 12, p. 49.

257 It is instructive here to remember the lamentation of Rousseau in the *Second Discourse*, since it constitutes the highest expression of the philosophical astonishment facing the two states of nature of man, the genuine one and the fallen one: "How shall man be able to see himself, such as nature formed him, in spite of all the alterations which a long succession of years and events must have produced in his original constitution, and how shall he be able to distinguish what is of his own essence, from what the circumstances he has been in and the progress he has made have added to, or changed in, his primitive condition?", Jean-Jaques Rousseau, "The Second Discourse: Discourse on the Origin and Foundations of Inequality Among Mankind," in *The Social Contract and The First and Second Discourses* (New Haven and London: Yale University Press, 2002), p. 81.

The second meaning – the first as importance, in Hobbes's doctrine – is in relation to the understanding of *human nature*[258] as an essence that repeats itself with every human individual, forasmuch he is, by birth, in the first place, an animal dominated by concerns and instincts, becoming social (but not sociable) only through education and calculation. When reminding man's unsocial nature and the need to subject him to discipline, Hobbes seems to consider mostly this situation. Even the most famous interpreters try to "overlook" this true paralogism of the state of nature, trying to solve it at all costs,[259] by Hobbes's means or by other.

By pointing out that the ambiguity of the state of nature isn't just present in Rousseau and Locke, but also in Hobbes, Macpherson demolishes the myth of the systematic character of the Hobbesian philosophy.[260] However, Macpherson suggests an original way of remedying the fundamental ambiguity of the state of nature in Hobbes. If the expression "state of nature of humanity" would designate the primitive man's psychology and behavior, these would anyway be impossible to understand. Every time we would try to isolate, by abstraction, the original behavior of the natural man, we would find the reasons and the

---

258 Apart from the well-known opposition between Hobbes and Rousseau, concerning the good or the evil nature of man, we draw attention to some of the differences, which are just as important. Namely, Rousseau processes the ambiguity of the concept of natural state in favor of the historicity of human nature, admitting that life in society has brought important changes the initial form of the human soul.

259 Michael Oakeshott denounces the obsession of interpreters with solving a series of obscure matters in Hobbes's philosophy. "Setting out with false expectations, [they] have been exasperated by the ambiguity with which Hobbes uses certain important words [...] and have gone on, in an attempt to understand his theory better than he understood it himself, to interpret it by extracting from his writings at least some consistent doctrine." Oakeshott, "Introduction to *Leviathan*", p. 68.

260 However, we must notice that the interpretation became more accurate when we take into consideration the state of nature in *Leviathan* only, as John Rawls did. According to Rawls, there are three meanings of the state of nature generally speaking, since "there are three possible interpretations of the social contract," but Hobbes is not concerned in *Leviathan* with all of them. "First, it is an account of what actually happened and of how the state actually was formed. This is not Hobbes's intention as I interpret him. A second, more plausible interpretation, for which there is a good deal of evidence in the text, is that he was attempting to give a philosophical account of how the state could arise. [...] Finally, a third possible interpretation I suggested is the following: Suppose that the great Leviathan actually exists already. [...] Hobbes is trying to urge us into accepting an existing effective Sovereign." Rawls, *Lectures on the History of Philosophy*, p. 34.

desires of the civilized man. Macpherson asserts that the state of nature is seen by Hobbes as the presence, in the natural individual, of some characteristics that actually belong to civilized man. Although it functions as a logical hypothesis, the concept of the natural condition of mankind must be understood, in Hobbes, from the perspective of its empirico-inductive genesis: "state of nature is a statement of the behaviour to which men as they now are, men who live in civilized societies and have the desires of civilized men, would be led if all law and contract enforcement were removed."[261] The state of nature in Hobbes is the actual state, without the sovereign, but as the idea of this state would be "a logical and not an historical hypothesis"[262] it follows that the hypothesis of the primitive man as object of the Hobbesian psychology is a non-sense. Macpherson also rejects the other meaning of the state of nature; this one is also not the essence discovered by eliminating from human psychology those accidental characteristics that were passed on to him by society: "in calling this hypothetical condition 'the state of nature' Hobbes makes it easy to misread it either as a condition historically prior to civil society or as a hypothetical condition deduced from men's 'natural' characteristics considered entirely apart from their socially acquired characteristics."[263] Hobbes would therefore keep, in his concept of state of nature, certain schemes of social behavior, which will allow him to reinvent society. This wouldn't just be limited to the presence, in the concept of the state of nature, of some elements that pertain to man's presence in society, but more so, Hobbes's man is the representative of a special type of society that Macpherson calls "possessive market society."[264]

Macpherson's arguments in support of the first thesis are the actual examples brought by Hobbes to illustrate people's natural fear from one another. Hereby, when a person leaves on a trip he arms himself and worries about the persons accompanying him, or when he goes to bed he carefully locks the doors of his house and puts his possessions under lock and key. Hobbes would hence look for the confirmation of the natural tendency of people to destroy one another in the observable behavior of the contemporaries. Another example would be

---

261 Macpherson, *Political Theory of Possessive Individualism*, p. 22. "[...] state of nature is the hypothetical condition in which men as they now are, with natures formed by living in civilized society, would necessarily find themselves if there were no common power able to overawe them all." Ibid., pp. 18–19.

262 Ibid., p. 21.

263 Ibid., p. 28.

264 For the difference between simple market society and fully (or possessive) market society, see Ibid., 51–60.

the one of the civil war that Hobbes lived and described and that proved a good occasion to see in the anarchic and violent actions of people the manifestation of the human nature: what the hobbesian psychology describes are not (mediated) signs of man's nature, but its direct manifestations. If Hobbes poisoned his British contemporaries with a metaphor that suggested savagery and primitivism it is because the violence of the civil war were taking place right in the middle of the civilized world. Therefore, in the *Leviathan*, nature and civilization were forced to keep an impossible relationship in order to attract the attention that there is no need to travel in America's forests to discover ferocity[265].

Macpherson observes that all the examples brought by Hobbes in order to explain the reason of the disruption between people are linked to the joint life: the competition for earnings, the distrust in others for personal safety, the desire of glory or reputation. These three causes of quarrel operate in any society, but they become destructive only when there is no common power to control them. The individual's behavior in in each of the three situations implies an overall evaluation of others, of the purposes that they pursue and of the means that they use and, therefore, it also implies the development of some general principles for action. "For every man looketh that his companion should value him, at the same rate he sets upon himself; and upon all signs of contempt, or undervaluing, naturally endeavours, as far as he dares [...] to extort a greater value from his contemners, by damage."[266]

The conduct imposed by the struggle for recognition cannot be thus separated from the representation of some instrumental values such as the power of others, the sizing of the means and the measurement of value. The natural individual is not deprived of reason, and reason is a calculation, therefore the general rules of prudence are known by the natural man. In this case, we can more easily understand Hobbes's idea that man has malicious intents by nature without being morally bad: "For although they have from nature, i.e. from their birth itself, from the fact that they are born animals, this characteristic, that they immediately want what pleases them and do whatever they can, in fear of anger, either to flee or to ward off the evils that treaten them, they are not normally thought to be evil on that account. For the passions [*affectus animi*] which arises from animal nature are not themselves evil, though the actions that proceed from them sometimes are, namely, when they are harmful and contrary to duty"[267]. The presence of the

265 In *this* sense, the concept of human nature in Hobbes is a polemical one, according to Leo Strauss.

266 Hobbes, *Leviathan*, chapter XIII, 5, p. 83 [61].

267 Hobbes, *On the Citizen*, Preface to the readers, p. 11.

laws of prudence and of the values that allow the appreciation of human relations indicate that Hobbes's state of nature does not describe the abstracted behavior of the primitive man or of the human animal. Civilization is always and everywhere present in Hobbes's works[268].

The arguments brought to support the second thesis consider mainly the definition that Hobbes gives to the power "of a man" as well as the conclusions derived from here. Hobbes first describes the power as a combination of means that a man has at his disposal in order to obtain a future good, and he deduces then the conclusion that the general inclination of all men is the perpetual desire to acquire and amplify their power, a desire to which only death put an end[269]. According to Macpherson, in order to understand the transition from the definition of power to its generalized consequence one needs several additional postulates regarding the problem of power. Namely, by "a man's power" Hobbes does not understand the quantity of means in absolute, but their "eminence", that is the superiority of these means or capacities in relation to the ones put at the disposal of others. For example, the enumeration of the most important forms of power which men can acquire, of what is "honorable" as Hobbes put it, is nothing more than an inventory of the elements that define competition in the market economy: the power that each man possesses is nothing more than merchandise offered up, like all things, for evaluation and trade on the competitive market.

According to Macpherson, this understanding of power as a relative quantity that is established through comparison leads to the conclusion that the power of a man is opposed by the power of all the others. As Hobbes said, "the power of one man resisteth and hindereth the effects of the power of another,"[270] power is to be defined as the excess of the power of one man above that of another. And if the powers are equal, they destroy each other. Hobbes's text rather indicates that it is about the opposition of all the others *that are after the same thing*, and not all the other members of society, but this does not change much our problem. The opposition between people who are after the same thing – we rather not forget the detail – can be from now on called "competition" in the sense of economic liberalism, because the idea of *value* is born from the confrontation of the means possessed by individuals who are after the same thing: "The value, or WORTH of a man, is as of all other things, his price; that is to say, so much as would be given

268 Macpherson, *Political Theory of Possessive Individualism*, p. 30.

269 Hobbes, *Leviathan*, chapter XI, p. 75.

270 Hobbes, *Elements of Law*, I, chapter 8, § 4, p. 26.

for the use of his power: and therefore is not absolute; but a thing dependent on the need and judgment of another. [...] And as in other things, so in men, not the seller, but the buyer determines the price. For let a man (as most men do) rate themselves at the highest value they can; yet their true value is no more than it is esteemed by others."[271] The enumeration in the *Leviathan* of the most important forms of power that people can possess, of what is "honorable" like Hobbes says, is nothing but an inventory of the characteristic traits of the competition from the market economy: the power that every man possesses is nothing but a merchandise offered[272], like any other thing, to evaluation and exchange on a competitive market. Any man is at the same time seller and buyer; he takes part in the general merchandise evaluation system. This type of analysis of power and value implies the presence, in Hobbes, of a social postulate; a simple psychological or physiological definition of power would not be enough to define value. The Hobbesian individual psychology is therefore *social*: the tendency of every human individual to perpetuate his movement represents a start for the domination problem.

At this point, Macpherson's subtle analysis is confronted by Leo Strauss' classic interpretation. Here is the presentation of the problem by Macpherson himself: "two views are possible, depending on the interpretation of some of Hobbes's statements. [...] In the other view, Hobbes was inconsistent. While he sometimes derived the opposition of powers from the postulate that some but not all men innately desire ever more, he also sometimes derived it from the single physiological postulate that all men innately desire ever more power over others. It is not disputed in the second view that Hobbes did state that only some men are innately immoderate; it is only asserted that he was inconsistent in so doing."[273]

The place in Hobbes which is subject to competing interpretations is the chapter XI[274] of *Leviathan*, where the author himself asserts that not all people are insane for power, but the moderate ones come to act like the others because of uncertainty. This assertion truly contradicts the general image of the natural man who would be "evil" and vain, and puts in difficulty the physiologist hypothesis that imagines civil society only through the mechanism of passions. Strauss'

271 Hobbes, *Leviathan*, chapter X, 16, p. 59 [42].

272 We note that Macpherson's interpretation confirms our own, according to which, in Hobbes, "a man's power" is synonymous to property in Locke, including all the means (specially the *work*) that individual *owns* in order to attain his purposes.

273 Macpherson, *Political Theory of Possessive Individualism*, pp. 40–41. We have reversed the order in which the two interpretations are presented.

274 Hobbes, *Leviathan*, chapter XI, 66 sq. [47].

interpretation seems to be put in a difficult position, but the problem still can be solved by showing that Hobbes attaches to men a rational and an irrational craving.

Macpherson, in return, does not grant that this argument can solve the problem: "Hobbes does indeed say that some men strive for ever more power naturally (which may well be called an irrational striving), and that some men seek more power only to protect the moderate delights and power that would satisfy them (which may well be called a rational striving); but it cannot be inferred from this that Hobbes was attributing the innate or irrational striving to all men. Strauss points also to the fact that Hobbes found the struggle for honour, or precedence over others, and recognition of this precedence, to be a universal characteristic of man. So he did, but he did not say this was innate in all men."[275] If we understand well, Macpherson introduces in the exam of the hobbesian political philosophy the well-known dilemma if human faculties or characters are innate or acquired. If they are innate, the hobbesian political theory remains without a solid foundation because one cannot derive the need of social contact and the social relations from the simple physics of passions. If they are acquired, as far as all people have similar behavior, needs and means, and a system of evaluating their relations while they are in a perpetual and universal competition, then Hobbes's description of the state of nature can have no another model than the "generalized market society"[276].

3.3 Moral and political obligation

Macpherson's interpretation allows us to see the theories formulated by Hobbes and Locke from a unifying perspective. It puts the two theories in a type of relation which, beyond the divergence of doctrines, can result in common issues. What matters is seeing to what extent the divergences between the two theories can be integrated in a type of reading which allows the highlighting of a common significance, both in terms of politics and in terms of morals. This point brings us back to analyzing the relation between political obligation and moral obligation. From the perspective of Macpherson's interpretation, the two theories are the expression of the liberal *economic* ideology. Usually, the interpreters of Hobbes and Locke discuss the two systems of political philosophy from the perspective of liberal *political* doctrine, meaning the opposition between absolute monarchy,

275 Macpherson, *Political Theory of Possessive Individualism*, p. 43.

276 According to Macpherson, Locke followed Hobbes all the way, since he has limited justice to the definition given to it by the contracting parties on the market.

which Hobbes promotes and parliamentary democracy, asserted by Locke. The merits of Macpherson's interpretation consist of having shown that, beyond the political aspect and the option for monarchy or democracy, the two philosophies are first grounded in the *social structure* of the 17th century English society and most of all, in the structure of the generalized market economy. Indeed, most times, analysts concerned with the works of Hobbes and Locke have lost sight of the fact that the contractualist model of society is based on an *economic model*[277]. Without a doubt there has always been an agreement between men, in relation to different purposes and circumstances, but the contract between two or more parties is a special kind of agreement, regarding the obligations which warrant the trade of goods or services. The "natural right school" was not named as such because man was perceived as having certain "rights", but because the privileged object of civil right (jurisprudence) actually consisted in the *obligations* which derive from a contract, and perceiving society as a generalized system of obligations justified the idea that basically, society *is* a contract[278].

Macpherson shares the opinion of Leo Strauss, who designates Hobbes as the first liberal thinker, the founder of individualism, yet, if Hobbes were indeed the first liberal thinker, this is mainly justified by the fact that he thought of power (individual power, not civil power) through the perspective of completely market society. This means that Hobbes's political theory (and that of Locke as well) is first of all a theory concerning the civil obligations which ensue from the social contract. Without a doubt, the issue of rights is a fundamental one, but once such a foundation is established, Hobbes's moral and political theory raised the issue of whether obligations ensue from a contract, meaning from the *transfer of right.* However, civil obligation (i.e. obeying sovereign power and laws) would not be legitimate and would hold no meaning if man were not accustomed to the idea of obligation or if this idea was not innate in man. As Locke will put it, the law of nature speaks to men in the language of obligation: "the law of nature obliges every one" and "where there is no law, there is no freedom."[279]

Although this axiom of liberal thinking is present in Hobbes's thought, Raymond Polin believes that Hobbes is not a liberal thinker: he is rather a

277 Foucault, *Society must be defended*, pp. 13–14.

278 As Leo Strauss states, the theory of the social contract is only bound to the issue of *natural rights* starting with Hobbes who was the first to raise the issue of legitimate government instead of perfect government. For this reason, Strauss sees in Hobbes the first liberal thinker, the founder of individualism.

279 Locke, *Two Treatises of Government,* p. 306. [Second Treatise, VI, 57].

philosopher of liberty[280]. According to Polin, Hobbes has never directly established a theory of political obligation. The central idea concerning the absolute character of sovereignty emphasizes the fact that, in Hobbes, the concept of obligation must not be understood in its modern sense. The term of obligation, used today, was created by Kant according to whom, through his sensibility, man belongs to the natural world of phenomena, and through his reason to the intelligible field of things themselves. While the first field pertains to necessity, the second one pertains to freedom. Kant said that the will of man is not naturally good, since it is subject to the pressures of sensibility and of wishes, meaning that it is a heteronomous will. For this reason, moral action is only possible by compelling volition through reason. The morality of man is therefore conditioned by the compelling of volition through a categorical imperative, but this obligation is still free, since the restriction is not exerted from the outside, but from the inside, and this can only be possible by virtue of the will. Therefore, in Kant, moral obligation is opposed to natural necessity, and is seen as an exercise of free will; moral obligation is not an exterior restraint and can only be achieved by each man individually, through his freedom to choose, therefore through his conscience. This theory is the opposite of Hobbes's.

For the author of the *Leviathan*, man is part of the system of the world, and the world functions according to immutable and necessary laws. According to the classical science of nature, a movement is free when it does not meet an obstacle, and the same goes for volition, which is made up of bodily strength, passions etc. Therefore, freedom and necessity are not necessarily opposed. Spinoza asserted, in the same century as Hobbes, that freedom and understanding necessity is the same thing, which meant that natural law is not incompatible with moral freedom. Hobbes defines natural laws as being "moral" and uses the expression "natural and moral law" often enough, since for him, natural and moral laws define the mores of the state of nature, which are rational. Therefore, obligation and necessity seem to be one and the same thing, which leads to the conclusion that obligation does not pertain to conscience. It refers to the exterior coercion; this is why Hobbes states that any understanding or convention among men is worthless unless it is warranted by a greater power, namely that of the sovereign.

On the other hand however, there are a series of affirmations about Hobbes according to which "there being no obligation on any man which ariseth not from some act of his own"[281]; "for no man is obliged by a covenant whereof he

280 Polin, *Dieu et les hommes*, p. 126.

281 Hobbes, *Leviathan*, chapter XXI, 10, p. 144 [111].

is not author."[282] These passages can be easily understood if we consider the civil state, because it is the only state in which we can speak of stable conventions. These conventions can be of a moral nature (concerning mores) or of a political nature, and the obligation associated with them will be both a moral and a political obligation. It is for this reason why "freedom means something different in society from what it does in nature."[283] However, some conventions exist in the state of nature as well, although they are not thought to be durable, and this means that we may speak of moral obligation in the state of nature as well. Such an obligation would be, for example, gratitude and if we consider the gratitude of the children towards their parents, we may say that it is of a permanent nature. According to Warender, the gratitude, which is by definition different from convention, must be also based on the consent, since consent is projected into the future[284] and it creates an obligation.[285] However, we must say that "the relation between obligation and gratitude is quite difficult to analyze because the term of 'obligation' has, in Hobbes, an ambiguous meaning."[286]

But the constraint by means of which an individual forces another, in order to obtain something from him, does not constitute an obligation, just like you are under no obligation to submit yourself to the power of a highway man; this is rather the definition of what is *not* an obligation. From what was just said, it can be understood that obligation and necessity are not the exact same thing; you might say that obligation is an *accepted necessity*. The consent given by the person has the power and the effect of a moral law; but this consent cannot be understood as the self-determination of will in a Kantian way. For example, if a thief threatens me and makes me hand over all that I have, at gunpoint, I obey, I consent; the obligation in this case does not come from the thief's power, nor from my autonomous will; it comes from the natural principle of self-preservation, to which consent is added. The latter is the recognition of the fact that, indeed, the threat made by the thief constitutes a peril, since I do

---

282 Ibid., chapter XVI, 6, p. 106 [81].

283 D. van Mill, "Hobbes' Theories of Freedom", *The Journal of Politics* 57 (1995): p. 458.

284 Warrender, *Political Philosophy of Hobbes*, pp. 51–52.

285 See also G. J. Schochet, "Thomas Hobbes on the Family and the State of Nature", *Political Science Quaterly* 82(1967): p. 444. According to Schochet, "the future consent of the child was probably derived from Hobbes's fourth law of nature, the law of gratitude." Ibid., p. 433.

286 Corneliu, Bilba, "The Parent-Child Relation in Hobbes: Beyond Private Life and Public Reason," *Research and Social Intervention (Revista de Cercetare și Intervenție Socială)*, 32 (2011): p. 178.

not poses sufficient strength to defend myself. If, on the contrary, I decide not to obey, but to defend myself, since I feel that I am stronger than the thief and might defeat him, the justification of my deliberate act is found in natural law as well, more precisely, in natural right[287], which allows me to defend myself. The two possibilities, which are both in accordance with natural law, show that natural law is not the object of a prior choice: either I obey, either I do not, but natural law is at no time dependent on my acceptance or refusal; it is necessary and independent from consent. Therefore, the necessity is grounded in natural law, but the obligation resides in my consent. For Hobbes, this consent is not deliberate, in sense of freedom of the conscience; the freedom of my act is grounded in natural necessity. Obligation pertains to necessity to the extent that freedom itself cannot be separated from the latter.

From the above example we can note that, if the issue of obligation involves consent, this consent can be given either in the case of a civil understanding/convention, either in the case of a natural situation, when the obligation ensues from natural law. In general, Hobbes's interpreters define as "political" man's obligation as a citizen or as a sovereign, and as "moral" the obligation which is derived from a natural situation (state). This distinction was necessary since the term of "moral" in use today corresponds, in the works of Hobbes, to both social mores – those relations among civilized people which make up the object of a conversion, which however, is not civil, like the habit of drinking tea at five o'clock – as well as the natural situations in which determining volition is done through natural law. The status of mores is pretty ambiguous, since they depend to a great extent on conventions and they do not have any direct link to natural law; on the other hand, they can be seen as an expression of attitudes and natural interests; civilization can be synonymous to the sum of mechanisms and of social laws by means of which people attain their natural purposes (like the unlimited growth of power), without having to resort to the means of the state of nature. In the absence of sociability, morals cannot be understood in other way.

If this interpretation is correct, it means that Hobbes does not exclude at all the possibility of non-civil conventions among men, which take place by virtue of nature, but not in the state of nature (because they are not durable). The fact

---

287 "[…] that every man, ought to endeavour peace, as far as he has hope of obtaining it; and when he cannot obtain it, that he may seek, and use, all helps, and advantages of war. The first branch of which rule, containeth the first, and fundamental law of nature; which is, to seek peace, and follow it. The second, the sum of the right of nature; which is, by all means we can, to defend ourselves." Hobbes, *Leviathan*, chapter XIV, 4, p. 117 [64].

that Hobbes did not insist upon this "secondary" aspect of social life was seen as a shortcoming by Locke, who, as we have seen, had to attribute particular importance to those conventions made in the state of nature, first of all in relation to property. At the same time, it is just as true that the premise for dealing with non-civil conventions is found in the Chapter 11 of the *Leviathan,* where Hobbes speaks of manners.

By "manners", Hobbes does not understand fine (good) manners or "decency of behaviour [...] but those qualities of mankind, that concern their living together in peace, and unity."[288] But, in this case, the title of the chapter *Of the Difference of Manners* is not justified. The first thing that we find out about the variety and about the difference of manners is the inclination, manifested by all men, of gaining more and more power, this being a desire that only ceases in death. Variety then refers to "competition for gaining riches" and to all the other desires to earn honors and prestige, which are common in all men. In fact, Hobbes does not speak about the qualities of individuals; he speaks about the *qualities of mankind.* This implies that he is actually speaking of foundations, of the "bases" for the diversity of manners, which could at the same time be "the bases" of all conventions concerning manners. We know for certain that Hobbes was by no means a stranger to the issue of "manners" as behavior exhibited in society.

In response to the criticisms of a renowned geometry professor from Oxford, Hobbes answers in a text called *Of Manners* that: "it is ill manners, in reprehending the truth, to send a man in a boasting way to your own errors. [...] it is ill manners to diminish the just reputation of worthy men after they be dead."[289] Or, in this respect, one could answer Hobbes, using the arguments of Chapter 11 of the *Leviathan* that the diversity of *mores* leaves plenty of space for the interpretation of *manners.* Still, one cannot answer in such a way, because in that particular chapter Hobbes speaks rather of what makes men similar in state of nature, and implicitly, of what could or should reunite them in civil society. But what unites people in civil society is not fine manners, it is fear of the sovereign's power. As a result, fine manners and all the other conventions are presented as ensuing from the social contract; they do not bear the mark of society, they are a rational artifice which tends to dissimulate human nature in order to leave room for diplomacy and for calculations. "In *Elements* 8.5, Hobbes presents the honors

---

288 Hobbes, *Leviathan*, chapter XI, 1, p. 65 [47]. We suggested this by using the term "mores", not "manners".

289 Thomas Hobbes, "Of Manners", In *The English Work of Thomas Hobbes of Malmesbury*, now first collected and published by Sir William Molesworth, vol. VII (London: John Bohn, 1845), p. 354.

that superior and inferior give one another as a strategic account, for the signs of honor 'the inferior giveth to the superior' are strategic responses to the signs of honor 'from the superior to the inferior'."[290] "Bad manners" then signify, in the light of the philosophy of the *Leviathan,* lack of civil spirit and braking with civil conventions. We realize that this conclusion is a tremendous error; which becomes all the more obvious since in his dispute with the reputed Oxford professor, Hobbes's only argument is that the professor has what is called ill-breeding. Going back to the theory of the *Leviathan,* ill-breeding should be interpreted as bad family upbringing, meaning a faulty transition from the state of nature to the civil state. Still, the difficulty resides in the fact that this transition should involve a social time and place for the good or bad upbringing to take place in. You might say that the biggest difficulty of the *Leviathan* resides in the fact that Hobbes does not speak of ill-manners or that he does not leave enough room to discuss those conventions which institute good manners.

Hobbes's interpreters grant this fact little importance; the difference between Hobbes and Locke has marked the understanding of this matter to such an extent that it is no longer noticeable that in the end, the development of Locke's theory took place by filling in the gaps left by the *Leviathan.* As far as we know, Locke is Hobbes's first and last interpreter to see and notice that the issue of morals does not have a solid foundation in the *Leviathan* and that it must be transferred to the effective state of nature in order to gain such a foundation. For Locke, this foundation will be represented by the non-civil conventions that people were able to establish among themselves in the state of nature, by virtue of natural law; this is what makes the hypothesis of sociability necessary. In specialized literature, authors insist a lot on the matter of property in Locke, but it isn't always made clear enough that aside from being a mere doctrine, the theory of property is, for Locke, the solution to a problem. Namely, it is the foundation of mores, of those manners to which Hobbes hadn't granted too much importance and which will form, not in the works of Locke, but in those of his followers, the matter of social civil society, seen as separate from the state. In order to illustrate the way in which the issue of mores has been set aside by Hobbes's interpreters, we will refer to a significant passage in the famous review made by Leo Strauss to the writing of Carl Schmitt, *The concept of the political.* Strauss said: "Hobbes understood the *status civilis* in the sense of the specifically modern concept of culture [...] as the opposite of the *status naturalis*; the *status civilis* is the presupposition of every culture in the narrow

290 Bilba, "The Parent-Child Relation", p. 186.

sense (i.e. every nurture of the arts and sciences) and is itself already based on a particular culture, namely, on a disciplining of the human will. We will here disregard Hobbes's view of the relationship between *status naturalis* and culture (in the broadest sense) as an opposition."[291] There is, in the case of Strauss, a certain ambiguity concerning the matter of culture, but this ambiguity must be attributed to Hobbes himself: the Leviathan is the condition of culture in the restricted sense, but even this work is based on a certain culture, in the broad meaning – let us not forget that the Leviathan was called by Hobbes "the artificial man", a man created by man in his own image, in the image of natural man. Thinking of the cultural status of the state, we realize that this condition should be both cultural and natural (in its broad sense), which is hard to imagine, given the opposition between the two. Therefore, Strauss – which dealt with the text from the perspective of the natural to the political and who wanted to reject Schmitt's thesis, which saw the condition of the political *directly* in nature (without the interposition of culture) – has to *make abstraction* of this opposition which cannot be qualified by the means devised by Hobbes. Apart from its shortcomings, Hobbes's merit consists, Strauss believes, in his "knowing and seeing against what the liberal ideal of civilization has to be persistently fought for: not merely against rotten institutions, against the evil will of a ruling class, but against the natural evil of man. In an unliberal world Hobbes forges ahead to lay the foundation of liberalism against the – *sit venia verbo* – unliberal nature of man, whereas later men [...] trust in the original goodness [...] of human nature. [...] But—in all fairness to later men – ultimately that dreaming and that oblivion are merely the consequence of the negation of the state of nature, merely the consequence of the position of civilization introduced by Hobbes."[292] Ambiguity is once more present: it is not clear enough whether, in Hobbes, the *moment* when nature is denied is equivalent to the assertion of civilization. Locke, who is Hobbes's first successor, was therefore right when placing the foundation of civilization – of mores – within state of nature itself, but we have already seen that his interpretation also has ambiguities. This deviation from the problem of obligation shows us just how difficult – or impossible – a theory of obligation actually is, but on the other hand, to what extent we need political theory to be preceded by a "science of manners". For Hobbes, there was no such a thing as a theory of manners, or as a foundation of such a theory, since he did not dispose of effective means to make these the object

291 Strauss, "Notes on Carl Schmitt", p. 105.
292 Strauss, "Notes on Carl Schmitt", pp. 107–108.

of a science. Mores are not universal, and Hobbes is interested only in that which is universal in moral philosophy (which encompasses both moral science and political science), without the universal being conditioned by the concepts of freedom and conscience which we latter find in Kant. In his work, *De cive,* Hobbes announces that the object of moral science is moral law or the law of nature, which for him are one and the same thing and which constitute the condition for natural justice. If the obligation is derived from natural law, it is an obligation towards nature: in the state of nature, it manifests itself as the will to preserve one's life. "There is no difference in nature between obligation and desire,"[293] satisfying one's needs in order to live is the result of an obligation of the natural law of self-preservation.

For this reason, in the state of nature, the war of all men against all men is outside the classifications of "good" and "bad", much like free competition between individuals – in the civil state – cannot be considered as morally negative. In fact, in the civil state, moral obligation also comes from natural law, by virtue of the fear inspired by the sovereign, who guarantees all other conventions. In this sense, mores have, as formal condition, the initial contract through which the sovereign gains the power to warrant all the other conventions, and, as efficient condition, the natural desire. Therefore, mores pertain, in a negative manner, to a double regimen: not in the sense that they are both civil and natural, but in the sense that they are neither civil, nor natural. At this point, we are faced with the ambiguity of the relation between nature and culture (in the broad sense) of which Leo Strauss spoke. Mores are rational strategies for action determined by natural volition; slyness, diplomacy, calculations, competition, desire (for more power) or purpose are just a few of their conditions, conditions which pertain to one of the three faculties which determine action: passion, reason and volition. Volition is nothing more than the sum of desires and of passions; reason consists of the very calculations which make up passions. In a very broad sense, will is determined by reason, the only problem being that reason does not constitute an autonomous reign in relation to nature. Still, determining will by the calculations of passions can be called moral and, in this respect, it makes sense to speak of moral obligation and of right: "moral designates a class of ways of life and actions. The term 'right' signifies nothing more than the freedom that each of us has to use his natural faculties, according to just reason."[294] The law of

293 Polin, *Hobbes, Dieu et les homes*, p. 159 [my translation].

294 Polin, *Hobbes, Dieu et les homes*, p. 159 [my translation]. See also *De cive* I, 7: "It is therefore neither absurd, nor reprehensible; neither against the dictates of true reason for a man to use all his endeavours to preserve and defend his Body, and the

nature is nothing more than the convergence between the game of passions and the calculations of reason: "reason is no less of the nature of man than passion, and is the same in all men."[295] The laws of nature are nothing more than reasoning, calculations born of reasoning starting from the premise of self-preservation (meaning the general law of nature); social contract is nothing more than the result of a calculation of our reason, meant to ensure the observance of the laws of nature, which would always be broken were it not for a power higher than any other which binds people to follow them. But this obligation which comes from the outside is in fact the obligation of natural law, since every individual *consents* to submit to the sovereign.

According to Hobbes, all men have the same nature, they possess the same faculties, are therefore equal, and their natural actions are the expression of a need which comes from the natural principle of self-preservation. But although everyone's reason can formulate and understand all the laws of nature which are derived from the principle of self-preservation, these laws remain "abstract", as Hegel[296] puts it, since the individual acknowledges them in his inner consciousness, yet does not acknowledge, by virtue of these laws, other people's right to freedom. The obligation that ensues from these laws for each individual (to seek and to follow peace, to give up his right and to be content with as much freedom as he would grant others, to follow conventions etc.) are not sufficient in order to achieve morality, since this obligation towards natural law only acts within ourselves. Obligation is constituted through conscience: "the Lawes of Nature had regard chiefly unto Conscience,"[297] but this cannot insure universality, because it is merely an opinion, a manner of judging which can prove to be wrong.

Several of Hobbes interpreters have demonstrated that not only moral or natural obligation, but also political obligation should be considered in retrospect to conscience: the Commonwelth must be based on the obligation of conscience[298]. If this was the case, it would mean either that human nature is "good", either that it becomes good in society. Hobbes's favorite example, civil

---

Members thereof from death and sorrowes; but that which is not contrary to right reason, that all men account to be done justly, and with right; Neither by the word Right is any thing else signified, then that liberty which every man hath to make use of his naturall faculties according to right reason." Hobbes, *De cive*, p. 47.

295 Hobbes, *Behemoth*, p. 87.

296 Hegel *Lectures on the History of Philosophy,* Vol. 2, pp. 167–169.

297 Hobbes, *De cive*, chapter IV, 21, p. 83.

298 F. C. Hood, *The divine Politics of Hobbes: An Interpretation of Leviathan* (Oxford: Clarendon Press, 1964), p. 123.

war, shows us that there is no need to interpret the *Leviathan* in Locke's philosophical spirit, and even less so in the spirit of Hegelian philosophy (which deal with universal consciousness). The idea of conscience in Hobbes is too close to the spirit of mechanisms to understand in such a manner the relation between morality and conscience. Hobbes is not far from Spinoza, for whom being aware of the effects is not the same as being aware of the causes, and man cannot be a primary cause (*causa sui*). In Hobbes, we cannot speak of the freedom of conscience as a free principle of action, even less so of a "political" universal conscience which would lead to the common interpretation of civil laws. According to other interpretations, in Hobbes, conscience is nothing more than an individual arbitrator: "In the state of nature, each individual is the judge concerning the best way to preserve his life, each individual's judgment and therefore each individual's conscience involves a natural obligation."[299] This affirmation made by R. Polin seems to be pretty close to the spirit of Hobbes, but "natural obligation" needs to be explained. As Michael Oakeshott points out in his famous *Introduction* to the 1946 edition of the *Leviathan*, "Under the influence of distinctions we are now accustomed to make in discussing questions of moral theory, modern critics of Hobbes have often made the mistake of looking for an order and coherence in his thoughts on these questions which is foreign to the ideas of any seventeenth-century writer. Setting out with false expectations, we have been exasperated by the ambiguity with which Hobbes uses certain important words (such as obligation, power, duty, forbid, command), and have gone on, in an attempt to understand his theory better than he understood it himself, to interpret it by extracting from his writings at least some consistent doctrine."[300] Talking into account these assignations, we come to the conclusion that the relation between "natural obligation" and conscience is far from resulting in a pertinent formulation of a theory about moral obligation in Hobbes, especially if we take into account the fact that the term "natural" doesn't just have one meaning. "Natural obligation" can, at the same time, refer to the physical necessity, to the physiological necessity or to the moral one (natural law). That which is added to physical necessity, in order to turn it into a physiological necessity, is the movement of passions, and that which is added to the physiological necessity in order to turn it into moral necessity is the calculation of reason, the result of which is volition. Hobbes only briefly defines conscience, and most of the time he uses the term as synonym for "consent". This term allows us to

299 Polin, *Hobbes, Dieu et les hommes*, p. 162.
300 Oakeshott, "Introduction to *Leviathan*", p. lviii.

understand that if a man consents to submit to an external coercion or to create a convention together with others, he creates an obligation. When speaking of self-preservation, obligation comes from the physical or physiological necessity, and all that reason does is to search for means of action; conscience is indeed an "arbitrary" arbitrator. Still, formulating the laws of nature is an act that the theory of an arbitrary conscience cannot explain: these laws are only universal *for man,* unlike the ("more" universal) principle of *self*-preservation, which is valid for any living thing. This implies that man possesses a universal faculty which allows him to know natural laws; this faculty is called reason. But if there is such a faculty which formulates the universal laws of nature, shouldn't there also be a universal principle which should make their fulfillment possible, at least in theory? We believe here is where the ambiguity of Hobbes's theory lies, concerning human nature: he cannot admit a faculty of action which would be universal ever since the state of nature, since this would make man good by nature. Still, he cannot let go of the idea of knowing natural laws by nature, since this would mean that the social contract is no longer possible. This is the same as saying that society is necessary and that it belongs to human nature as its last consequence. In Hobbes, we can speak of man's "sociable unsociability": once natural laws become known, natural obligation can be called moral obligation, since the laws of nature assign a certain content for human behavior: to seek peace, to concede right, to follow conventions. Moral law can be identified with natural law only through the fact that it could determine a universal natural obligation. The law of self-preservation tends to become the foundation of morality once we may speak of the self-preservation of all. This may become possible by virtue of reason, meaning of the other natural laws which are derived from the principle of self-preservation. Since these laws are eternal, the obligation which they bring about is also eternal, and therefore also valid in the state of nature, the difference being that in the state of nature the obligation exists in the conscience, but it is not effective. In order for it to become effective, meaning truly universal, a civil convention is needed. In society, the observance of natural laws is ensured by the positive laws which constitute "a sort of public conscience.[301]

301 Polin, *Hobbes, Dieu et les hommes*, p. 162.

References

Angoulvent, Anne-Laure. *Hobbes et la morale politique*. Paris: Presses Universitaires de France, 1994.

Aquinas, Saint Thomas. *Summa theologica*. Christian Classic Ethereal Library. http://www.ccel.org/ccel/aquinas/summa.pdf.

Aristotle. "Politics". Translated by Benjamin Jowett. In *Complete Works of Aristotle*, vol. 2, edited by Jonathan Barnes, 1017–1191. Princeton (N.J.): Princeton University Press, 1991.

Ashford, Elizabeth and Mulgan, Tim. "Contractualism." In *The Stanford Encyclopedia of Philosophy*, edited by Edward N. Zalta. http://plato.stanford.edu/archives/fall2012/entries/contractualism/. (Fall 2012 Edition).

Baumrin, B. "Hobbes's egalitarim: The laws of natural equality". In *Thomas Hobbes, de la méthaphysique à la politique*, Collque franco-americain de Nantes, sous la direction de Martin Bertman et Michel Malherbe, 119–125. Paris: Vrin, 1989.

Bilba, Corneliu. "The Parent-Child Relation in Hobbes: Beyond Private Life and Public Reason". *Research and Social Intervention (Revista de Cercetare și Intervenție Socială)* 32 (2011): 172–193.

Bilba, Corneliu and Gabriela Ratulea. "Suveranitate și violență la Hobbes și Foucault". In *Violența. Aspecte psihosociale*, editat de Gilles Ferréol și Adrian Neculau, 17–33. Iași: Polirom, 2003.

Campagna, N. *Thomas Hobbes. L'ordre et la liberté*. Paris: Michalon, 2000.

Cicero. "On the Laws". In Cicero, *On the Commonwealth and On the Laws*, edited by James E. G. Zetzel, 1–103. Cambridge: Cambridge University Press, 1999.

Clausewitz, Carl von. *On War*. Edited and Translated by Michael Howard and Peter Paret. New Jersey: Princteton University Press, 1989.

Constant, Benjamin. *Principes de politique applicables à tous les gouvernements*. Paris, Hachette, 1997.

Cudd, Ann. "Contractarianism." In *The Stanford Encyclopedia of Philosophy*, edited by Edward N. Zalta. http://plato.stanford.edu/archives/win2013/entries/contractarianism/ (Winter 2013 Edition).

Dyzenhaus, David, "Hobbes on the Authority of Law." In *Hobbes and the Law*, edited by David Dyzenhaus and Thomas Poole, 186–209. Cambridge: Cambridge University Press, 2012.

Foisneau, Luc. *Politique, Droit et Théologie chez Bodin, Grotius et Hobbes*. Paris: Kimé, 1997.

Foucault, Michel. *Society must be defended: Lecture at the College de France, 1975–76*. Edited by Mauro Bertani and Alessandro Fontana. Translated by David Macey. New York: Picador, 2003.

Gaius. *Gai Institutiones or Institutes of Roma Law*. Translated by Edward Poste. Oxford: Clarendon Press, 1904.

Gauthier, David. *The Logic of Leviathan: the Moral and Political Theory of Thomas Hobbes*. Oxford: Clarendon Press, 1969.

Gauthier, David. "Hobbes on Demonstration and Construction." *Journal of the History of Philosophy*, 35(1997): 509–521.

Grotius, Hugo. *The Rights of War and Peace: Book I*. Edited and with an Introduction by Richard Tuck, [translated by John Morrice (1715/1738)]. Indianapolis: Liberty Fund, 2005.

Halperin, Jean-Louis. *Legal Interpretation in 18th Century Europe: Doctrinal Debates Versus Political Change*. In *Interpretation of Law in the Age of Enlightenment: From the Rule of the King to the Rule of Law*, edited by M. Yasutomo et al., 107–124. Dordrecht: Springer, 2011.

Harrison, Ross. *Hobbes, Locke, and Confusion Masterpiece: An Examination of Seventeenth-Century Political Philosophy*. Cambridge: Cambridge University Press, 2003.

Hayek. F. A. *Individualism and Economic Order*. Chicago: The University of Chicago Press, 1984.

Hegel, G. W. F. *Lectures on natural right and political science: the first philosophy of right: Heidelberg, 1817–1818, with additions from the lectures of 1818–1819*. Translated by J. M. Stewart and P. C. Hodgson. Berkeley and Los Angeles: University of California Press, 1995.

Hegel, G.W.F. *Lectures on the History of Philosophy: Volume 2: Plato and the Platonists*. Translated by E.S. Haldane and Frances H. Simson. Lincoln: University of Nebraska Press, 1995.

Hobbes, Thomas. "Behemoth, the history of the causes of the civil war of England." In *The English Work of Thomas Hobbes of Malmesbury*, collected and published by Sir William Molesworth, vol. VI. London: John Bohn, 1840.

Hobbes, Thomas. "Of Manners." In *The English Work of Thomas Hobbes of Malmesbury*, now first collected and published by Sir William Molesworth, vol. VII, 331–365. London: John Bohn, 1845.

Hobbes, Thomas. *De cive: The English Version*. A critical edition by Howard Warrender. Oxford: Oxford University Press, 1983.

Hobbes, Thomas. *Man and Citizen (De Homine and De Cive)*. Edited by Bernard Gert. Translated by Charles T. Wood. Indianapolis: Hacket Publishing Company, 1991.

Hobbes, Thomas. *The Elements of Law Natural and Politic*. New York: Oxford University Press, 1994.

Hobbes, Thomas. *Leviathan*. Edited with an Introduction and Notes by J. C. A. Gaskin. Oxford: Oxford University Press, 1998.

Hood, F. C. *The divine Politics of Hobbes: An Interpretation of Leviathan*. Oxford: Clarendon Press, 1964.

Hobbes, Thomas. *On the Citizen*. Edited and translated by Richard Tuck and Michael Silverthorne. Cambridge: Cambridge University Press, 2003.

Hoekstra, Kinch. "Hobbes on the Natural Condition of Mankind." In *The Cambridge Companion to Hobbes's Leviathan*, edited by Patricia Springborg, 109–127. Cambridge: Cambridge University Press, 2007.

Janet, P. *Histoire de la science politique dans ses rapports avec la morale*. Paris: Alcan, 1887.

Johns, Christopher Lowell. *The Science of Right in Leibniz's Practical Philosophy*. New York: Bloomsbury, 2013.

Jouffroy, Th. *Cours de droit naturel*. Paris : Fayard, 1998.

Kant, Immanuel. "Toward Perpetual Peace: A Philosophical Sketch." In *Toward Perpetual Peace and Other Writings on Politics, Peace, and History*, by Immanuel Kant, edited and with an introduction by Pauline Kleingeld, translated by David L. Colclasure, 67–109. New Haven and London: Yale University Press, 2006.

Leibniz, G.W., "Opinion on the Principles of Pufendorf (1706)." In *Leibniz's Political Writings*, edited by Patrick Riley, 64–75. Cambridge: Cambridge University Press, 1988.

Lloyd, S.A. *Morality in the Philosophy of Thomas Hobbes: Cases in the Law of Nature*. Cambridge: Cambridge University Press, 2009.

Lloyd, Sharon A., and Sreedhar, Susanne. "Hobbes's Moral and Political Philosophy." In *The Stanford Encyclopedia of Philosophy*, edited by Edward N. Zalta, http://plato.stanford.edu/archives/spr2014/entries/hobbes-moral/ (Spring 2014 Edition).

Locke, John. *Two Treatises of Government and A Letter Concerning Toleration.* Edited and with an Introduction by Ian Shapiro. New Haven and London: Yale University Press, 2003.

Locke, John. *Two Treatises of Government.* Edited with an introduction and notes by Peter Laslett. Cambridge: Cambridge University Press, 1988.

Macpherson, Crawford Brought. *The Political Theory of Possessive Individualism: Hobbes to Locke.* Oxford and New York: Oxford University Press, 1962.

Manent, Pierre. *An Intellectual History of Liberalism.* Translated by Rebecca Balinski. Princeton: Princeton University Press, 1996.

Manent, Pierre. *Naissance de la politique moderne: Machiavel/Hobbes/Rousseau.* Paris: Editions Payot, 1977. [Consulted in Romanian translation: Manent, Pierre. *Originea politicii moderne.*

Machiavelli/Hobbes/Rousseau. Traducere de Alexandra Ionescu. Bucuresti: Editura Nemira, 2000].

Martinich, A.P. *Hobbes: A Biography.* Cambridge: Cambridge University Press, 1999.

Maurois, André. *A History of England.* Translated by Hamish Miles. London: Jonathan Cape, 1937.

Oakeshott, Michael. "Introduction to *Leviathan.*" In *Hobbes on Civil Association,* by Michael Oakeshott, 1–79. Indianapolis: Liberty Fund, 1975.

Parkin, Jon. *Taming the Leviathan: The Reception of the Political and Religious Ideas of Thomas Hobbes in England 1640–1700.* Cambridge: Cambridge Univesity Press, 2007.

Pateman, C. "God Hath Ordained to Man a Helper': Hobbes, Patriarchy and Conjugal Right." *British Journal of Political Science,* 19(1989): 445–463.

Polin, Raymond. *Hobbes, Dieu et les hommes.* Paris: Presses Universitaires de France, 1981.

Pufendorf, Samuel. "On the Law of Nature and of Nations." In *The Political Writings of Samuel Pufendorf,* edited by Craig L. Carr, 95–268. Oxford: Oxford University Press, 1994.

Pufendorf, Samuel. *The Whole Duty of Man According to the Law of Nature.* Translated by Andrew Tooke (1691). Edited with an Introduction by Ian Hunter and David Saunders. Indianapolis: Liberty Fund, 2003.

Rawls, John. *A Theory of Justice.* Cambridge (MA): The Belknap Press of Harvard University Press, 1999.

Rawls, John. *Lectures on the History of Political Philosophy*. Edited by Samuel Freeman. Cambridge (MA): The Belknap Press of Havard University Press, 2007.

Ross, W. D. *Aristotle*. London and New York: Routledge, 2005.

Rousseau, Jean-Jacques. "The Social Contract." In *The Social Contract and The First and Second Discourses*, by Jean-Jacques Rousseau, edited by Susan Dunn, 149–255. New Haven and London: Yale University Press, 2002.

Rousseau, Jean-Jacques. "The Second Discourse: Discourse on the Origin and Foundations of Inequality Among Mankind." In *The Social Contract and The First and Second Discourses*, edited by Susan Dunn, 69–148. New Haven and London: Yale University Press, 2002.

Schochet, G. J. "Thomas Hobbes on the Family and the State of Nature". *Political Science Quaterly* 82(1967): 427–445.

Schmitt, Carl. *The Leviathan in the State Theory of Thomas Hobbes: Meaning and Failure of a Political Symbol*. Translated by George Schwab and Erna Hilfstein. Westport and London: Greenwood Press, 1996.

Sellers, Mortimer N. S. "What Is the Rule of Law and Why Is It So Important?" In *The Legal Doctrines of the Rule of Law and the Legal State (Rechtsstaat)*, edited by James R. Silkenat, James E. Hickey Jr., Peter D. Barenboim, 3–14. Dordrecht: Springer, 2014.

Sommerville, Johann. "Lofty Science and Local Politics." In *The Cambridge Companion to Thomas Hobbes*, edited by Tom Sorell, 246–273. Cambridge: Cambridge University Press, 1996.

Socaciu, E. *Filosofia politica a lui Thomas Hobbes*. Iasi: Editura Polirom, 2001.

Sorell, Tom, ed. *The Cmabridge Companion to Thomas Hobbes*. Cambridge: Cambridge University Press, 1996.

Spinoza, Benedict. *Theological-Political Treatise*. Edited by Jonathan Israel, translated by Michael Silverthorne and Jonathan Israel. Cambridg: Cambridge University Press, 2007.

Stolleis, Michael. "Judicial Interpretation in Transition from the Ancien Régime to Constitutionalism." In *Interpretation of Law in the Age of Enlightenment: From the Rule of the King to the Rule of Law*, edited by M. Yasutomo et al., 3–20. Dordrecht: Springer, 2011.

Strauss, Leo. *The Political Philosophy of Hobbes: Its Basis and Its Genesis*. Translated from the German Manuscript by Elsa M. Sinclair. Chicago and London: The University of Chicago Press, 1963.

Strauss, Leo. *Natural Right and History*. Chicago: The University of Chicago Press, 1965.

Strauss, Leo. "Notes on Carl Schmitt, 'The Concept of the Political.'" Translated by J. Harvey Lomax. In *The Concept of the political*, by Carl Schmitt, translated and with an Introduction by George Schwab, with a Foreword by Tracy B. Strong, and Notes by Leo Strauss, 99–122. Chicago and London: The University of Chicago Press, 2007.

Sullivan, Vickie. *Machiavelli, Hobbes, and the Formation of a Liberal Republicanism in England*. Cambridge: Cambridge University Press, 2004.

Van Mill, D. "Hobbes' Theories of Freedom". *The Journal of Politics* 57(1995): 443–459.

Warrender, Howard. *The Political Philosophy of Hobbes: His Theory of Obligation*. Oxford: Oxford University Press, 1957.

Weber, Max. "The Profession and Vocation of Politics." In *Political Writings*, edited by Peter Lassman and Ronald Speirs, 309–369. Cambridge: Cambridge University Press, 1994.

Weil, Eric. *Philosophie politique*. Paris : Vrin, 1996.

www.ingramcontent.com/pod-product-compliance
Ingram Content Group UK Ltd.
Pitfield, Milton Keynes, MK11 3LW, UK
UKHW041829100926
8556IPUK00002B/92

9 783631 665503